Sisters & Brothers

FOREVER

H. NORMAN WRIGHT

Regal

A Division of Gospel Light
Ventura, California, U.S.A.

Published by Regal Books
A Division of Gospel Light
Ventura, California, U.S.A.
Printed in U.S.A.

Regal Books is a ministry of Gospel Light, an evangelical Christian publisher dedicated
to serving the local church. We believe God's vision for Gospel Light is to provide church
leaders with biblical, user-friendly materials that will help them evangelize, disciple and
minister to children, youth and families.

It is our prayer that this Regal book will help you discover biblical truth for your own life
and help you meet the needs of others. May God richly bless you.

For a free catalog of resources from Regal Books and Gospel Light please call your Christian supplier,
or contact us at 1-800-4-GOSPEL or at www.gospellight.com.

All Scripture quotations, unless otherwise indicated, are taken from the *Holy Bible, New International
Version*®. *NIV*®. Copyright © 1973, 1978, 1984 by International Bible Society. Used by permission
of Zondervan Publishing House. All rights reserved.

Other versions used are:

AMP.—Scripture taken from THE AMPLIFIED BIBLE, Old Testament copyright ©
1965, 1987 by the Zondervan Corporation. The Amplified New Testament © 1958,
1987 by The Lockman Foundation. Used by permission.

NASB—Scripture taken from the *New American Standard Bible*, © 1960, 1962, 1963,
1968, 1971, 1972, 1973, 1975, 1977 by The Lockman Foundation. Used by permission.

NEB—From *The New English Bible*. © The Delegates of Oxford University Press and The
Syndics of the Cambridge University Press 1961, 1970, 1989. Reprinted by permission.

NKJV—From the *New King James Version*. Copyright © 1979, 1980, 1982 by Thomas
Nelson, Inc. Publishers. Used by permission. All rights reserved.

RSV—From the *Revised Standard Version* of the Bible, copyright 1946, 1952, and 1971 by
the Division of Christian Education of National Council of the Churches of Christ in
the USA. Used by permission.

THE MESSAGE—Scripture taken from *THE MESSAGE*. Copyright © 1993, 1994, 1995
by Eugene H. Peterson. Used by permission of NavPress Publishing Group.

TLB—Verses marked (*TLB*) are taken from *The Living Bible* © 1971. Used by permission
of Tyndale House Publishers, Inc., Wheaton, IL 60189. All rights reserved.

Cover Design by Kevin Keller
Interior Design by Rob Williams
Edited by Kathi Mills and Deena Davis

Library of Congress Cataloging-in-Publication Data
Wright, H. Norman.
      Sisters and brothers forever / H. Norman Wright.
             p.   cm.
      Includes bibliographical references.
      ISBN 0-8307-2492-3 (hardcover).
      1. Brothers and sisters—Religious aspects—Christianity.
      2. Sibling rivalry. 3. Sibling abuse.   I. Title.
BF723.S43W75   1998
155.9'24—dc21   99-18217
                                                                                        CIP

Rights for publishing this book in other languages are contracted by Gospel Literature International
(GLINT). GLINT also provides technical help for the adaptation, translation and publishing of Bible
study resources and books in scores of languages worldwide. For further information,
contact GLINT, P.O. Box 4060, Ontario, CA 91761-1003, U.S.A. You may also send E-mail to
Glintint@aol.com, or visit their website at www.glint.org.

CONTENTS

Chapter One

Bond or Bondage?

In the 1960s when I was the youth pastor of a church in Southern California, a group of our college students occasionally would go to a small supper club that featured live entertainment. They especially enjoyed a new act made up of two musically gifted comedians who just happened to be brothers. Within a couple of years these brothers were performing on television. A few years later they hosted their own weekly TV series.

These well-known brothers were none other than Dick and Tommy Smothers. Part of their continuing comedy routine was Tommy saying to Dick, "Mom always liked you best," and then Dick replying, "Oh, she did not." Tommy would then counter, "Oh, yes, she did," and give some ridiculous reason for making that claim. Audiences loved it—it was great fun. Why? They identified with it. They'd been there. Many recognized it, to one degree or another, in their own lives.

We all have many significant people in our lives—or, at least, many people we consider significant. But for most of us, there is at least one highly significant person who cast a lasting shadow over our lives in some way, just as we have in his or her life. That person is not someone we dated for several years, or someone we worked with, or even the person we married. It's not even one of our parents, as influential as they were. This significant someone is our sibling—a brother or a sister.

It may be new territory for you to consider how a sibling has shaped your life. Many adults in our country and in Europe have at least one sibling with whom they often spend more time during formative childhood years than with their parents. Your sibling relationships have the potential to be the longest of any of your lifetime relationships. Sibling connections usually outlast those with parents by 20 to 30 years.

THROUGH THICK AND THIN

We can choose our friends, but friendship is not a lifetime guarantee. There are no binding contracts that can't be broken. Friends may come and go, when they move away, die or go on to new friendships.

Unfortunately, marriage doesn't always last either. Too many marriages die a painful death.

Connections with siblings may be the only intimate connections that last. Sibling relationships continue for better or for worse. Your brother will always be your brother, and your sister will always be your sister.

Siblings can be there for each other as the rest of the family diminishes in size. We usually can count on them to be around to share some of the latter part of our lives. And our siblings will always be our links to the past. Some sibling relationships remain close, while others drift apart. How close we were while growing up usually determines more than anything else how close we will be in later life.

These relationships are clearly evident and illustrated all around us—from Cain and Abel in the Bible to Hansel and Gretel in children's stories. Yet, in our society, we have taken sibling relationships for granted. Other societies place much more value upon the sibling relationship. In fact, there are some cultures where brother kinship is more important than parental kinship, and where the brothers make the decisions for the families.

Have you ever shared stories about yourself and your siblings with others who have siblings? If so, you probably discovered you had a lot in common! We all do, if we have brothers or sisters. But sadly, we have ignored the importance of these relationships for too long. Most of the time we hear about a mother's influence on her son or a dad's impact on his daughter, or just the opposite. But the influence of our siblings on who we are today is as strong, if not more so, than our parents' influence.

Vertical and Horizontal Relationships

As we grow from childhood to adulthood we have two directions in our relationships: vertical with our parents, and horizontal with our siblings. In the vertical relationship with our parents, we're always looking up to them. They establish—or fail to establish—the limits, the rules, the morals, the values. Children are supposed to respect, honor and obey their parents. Our parents help to shape our character, our values, our goals, defenses and coping mechanisms. Parents are authority figures. With them there are limits to what we can say and do. They are on a higher level than children. They have the edge in power and control, and they play by adult rules. They are the generals, giving orders to their subordinates. They have the lead in the opera, while children sing in the chorus.

In talking with a counselee about her family, I said, "You

need to remember, you weren't born to the same parents as your brothers and sisters."

There was a long silence while she looked at me with a strange expression. "I don't believe I'm hearing you correctly," she said. "Of course we have the same parents. If we didn't, we wouldn't be brothers and sisters."

I replied, "Think about it with me for a minute. You and your siblings had the same parents biologically, that's a fact. But no sibling is born to the same set of parents." I went on to tell her about what took place in the Jones family.

The first baby, John, was born to parents who were a bit nervous and edgy with him, since parenting was a new experience. They wanted to do their best and tended to hover. Because John's parents had been married for just two years, they were still very much in love. They both worked and were diligent about making and saving money. Although they wished they had more time to spend with John, they were comfortable with their childcare arrangements. They believed that children should conform to the schedule parents set, so John was fed according to their timetable.

As a result, John tended to be a bit cautious, taking on the characteristics of nervous, edgy parents, and he didn't like to take many chances. He had a healthy view of the importance of hard work and money and was comfortable fitting into schedules. No wonder!

Jean was the second child, born six years later. Jean's parents were more relaxed around her and more permissive in their child-rearing techniques. Her mother wasn't employed anymore, so she had more time with Jean than she had with John. However, Jean's parents had been married for eight years and had encountered the "Seven-Year Itch." The romance had gone out of their marriage and they were struggling.

In addition to these differences, we can't discount the effect of genes. John's genetic makeup gave him a compliant nature from the minute he entered the world. Jean came in fighting and independent. Is it any surprise that John and Jean received different responses from their parents?

Ken was the third child, born four years after Jean. Not only were Ken's parents relaxed with him, but as he got older, John and Jean helped out with some of his care. Ken watched how his parents responded to his brother and sister and consequently avoided some of their mistakes. Since Ken had to compete for his parents' attention (his mother had once again returned to work, and they were really on the career fast-track by this time), he learned how to be adaptable and clever. After all, he was a member of a family of five, whereas John had his parents all to himself before Jean came along and took away much of the attention he had been used to.

Three children with the same parents, but each had a different variation of these parents.

Often we look at how a person responds in life or what he does with his life, and we see it as an influence of the parents— or perhaps even a reaction against them. In some cases this may be true. There is another possibility. Consider the woman who has been married and divorced three times. Each husband seems to come from the same mold—charming, exciting, outgoing, irresponsible and untrustworthy.

In explaining her choice of husbands, many would say to look at the relationship between this woman and her father. What was the father like? There may be merit in this approach, but we don't want to stop with her father. Let's look a bit further. Each of these men was actually a replica of her younger brother. Was this a coincidence? Could it be there's more sibling influence here than father influence?

Consider the male executive vice president who is highly

regarded and competent. Now and then he has an opportunity to apply for an opening in a top position in one of the divisions of his company. It's obvious he could handle the work. Others even encourage him to follow through. Yet, he hesitates, as if he has some unknown blockage or fear.

Some might speculate about the reason in the following ways:

- His father probably pushed him into being the best when he was younger, and this is his way of rebelling.
- One of his parents probably said he'd never amount to much when he grew up, and now it's a self-fulfilling prophecy.
- He's a perfectionist and isn't sure how successful he'd be, so he's afraid of taking that step.
- He's a second-born child. His brother always excelled and had the limelight. Perhaps he stops himself because he feels that only his older brother could fill such a position.

Would you have considered this last possibility? You should, since it could very well be true.

There are many reenactments in the ongoing drama of life that have their roots with our parents. But we also have the sibling relationship, a horizontal relationship that has more influence upon us than most of us realize.

Think about the possibilities. Siblings have a greater freedom with one another than with their parents. They can be more open and honest with each other. They spend more time together than with their parents. They know one another in ways the parents will never know them. They learn what makes their siblings tick, how to upset them, how to get their approval and how to outdo them. They seem to have a greater level of intuitive response to their siblings than a parent may have. Some siblings have a higher degree of perceptiveness. They know when to empathize, what the siblings may be thinking, how to control them and how to activate their insecurities.

> *Parents are models but so are siblings.*
> *How else would we learn to play, work*
> *and even conflict with peers on a daily*
> *and often intense level?*

In each person's life there is a laboratory of sorts, similar to a research lab, where experiments and discoveries are made in an effort to better equip us for life. Part of those laboratory experiments and discoveries, in which interpersonal skills are tested and then either discarded or locked in for life, are conducted in conjunction with our siblings. Parents are models, but so are siblings. How else would we learn to play, work and even conflict with peers on a daily and often intense level?

Siblings learn how and when to defend one another, how and when to make the other look guilty, how and when to get along. Siblings get into some intense conflicts and fights. Sometimes parents wonder if they'll ever learn to get along. At times siblings are like a divisive army, battling each other and then, just as quickly, battling together against the outside world.

A friend of mine shared how he and his brother fought for years. He was the oldest of six children. The next child was a brother, 18 months younger. They fought about everything. When they were in high school, his younger brother was larger than he. One day they were fighting in the kitchen, and his brother hit him in the chest. It knocked the air out of him, and he fell to the floor, gasping for air. Suddenly his mother started to sob. Neither of them had ever seen their mother cry like that. It shocked them so much they never fought again. Instead, they developed a friendship. This happened more than 30 years ago, but my friend can still see it in his mind as if it happened yesterday.

Differing Sibling Relationships

Sibling relationships vary in closeness and distance within the same family. In a family of four siblings, two may be extremely close and the other two distant acquaintances. In another family, all four are inseparable. Distant relationships can be just as rigid as close ones.

There are three main groups of sibling relationships, and these are called patterns of identification. The first is known as close identification. In close identification, the sibling feels a strong similarity with, and very little difference from his or her sibling. Does this describe any relationship you have had or are experiencing now with one of your siblings?

Other siblings have only a partial identification, in which the sibling feels some similarity to as well as some distance from a sibling. Do you feel you have a partial identification relationship with one of your siblings?

Finally, there are those who have only distant identification. Very little similarity is felt in these relationships, but differences abound. Does distant identification seem to describe your relationship with one of your siblings?

VARYING DEGREES OF CLOSENESS

There are various possibilities of how close or distant relationships can be. Some siblings say, "You can't tell us apart. There's no difference. We're just like each other." In some families, because the roles are unclear, some siblings are almost fused. They share too much and find it difficult to function on their own. Unfortunately, their identity is together rather than separate.

I've seen others whose demeanors seem to say, "I'm not sure who I am; maybe I can be you." If children grow up without a clear, strong identity, they constantly search for someone to identify with. They may cling to another sibling. At times they may be close and then back off, but they are usually in doubt as to their own identity. Relationships get blurred.

Some siblings are caught up in hero worship. They make statements like, "I admire you so much, I want to become like you." This usually occurs between younger and older siblings. These siblings' lives are described as being copycats. What the other has or is, the copycat wants, and tries to emulate.

This can be good in some ways if the model has positive character traits. It's not unusual for people to idealize others and then identify with that perception in order to incorporate it into their own lives. If the older sibling is rebellious and constantly gets into trouble, this can be exciting to a younger sibling, who is then tempted to copy the behavior. Or, if a parent dies, younger children may find themselves without a role model, leaving them susceptible to becoming dependent on older siblings. Hopefully, by the time someone passes through adolescence, the person can establish his or her own identity.

A less intense variation of this sort of copycat identity is when children feel only some aspects of their personality are similar to those of a sibling. It could be something like, "We look the same," "We're both athletic," "We're both interested in conservation," "We're both loyal to our parents."

Some sibling relationships are mutually dependent—there is

give and take. The mutually dependent sibling says, "In our family, my sister and I are the same in many ways. There are some differences, but in spite of those differences, we'll always be there for each other." This is healthy and can be very fulfilling in adulthood.

Then we come to the ideal sibling relationship. This is reflected in the statement, "We're alike and we're different. This is a good thing. It presents challenges and growth, and opportunities for both of us." This is a balanced relationship. Each person has the freedom to develop his or her uniqueness while respecting but being challenged by the other. In a sense, each sibling is contrasted with the other. There is no clinging or contempt. The idea of being alike yet different, and that it's okay to be that way, is good preparation for marriage later on. Neither sibling wants to control or feel controlled, which of course would put the relationship out of balance.

HOSTILE RELATIONSHIPS

There are other relationships that aren't so healthy, such as the hostile dependent relationship. In this sort of relationship, the siblings say, "We're different in many ways. Not only that, we don't particularly like each other; and we don't need each other." There may be a toleration of one another, but each would prefer not to have contact with the other. Sometimes a sibling continues the relationship just to have someone to dump on. Siblings in a hostile dependent relationship don't help or support one another, and bitterness grows over the years.

It gets worse. Some siblings have a relationship characterized by "We're so different, how can we be related? I don't want to depend on you, and I never want to become like you!" These are siblings who may be very adept at keeping ledgers. Hurts and abuses are recorded and frozen in memory. Each may keep building a case against the other. Each acts as a creditor and debtor toward the other. These relationships sometimes occur because of abuse in the home. Some siblings have even been oppressed or brutalized by another. It's no wonder they feel as they do.

The most extreme of all sibling relationships is de-identification: "We're totally different. I don't need my sibling. I don't like him, and I don't ever want to see him again." While most siblings do identify with one another in some way, some choose to de-identify, expressing a denial of any similarity and a desire to extract the other from his or her life. When a sibling feels this way, chances are he or she never protects the other, condemning and avoiding the other sibling if possible. The relationship between siblings who de-identify is best expressed by, "Get away from me." These siblings determine not to become like one another.

Re-Creating the Familiar

Most of us have had experiences with a sibling that have been seared into our minds in one way or another—some good, some not so good. What are some of your memories? How have these influenced your life?

As I said earlier, the way we interact and get along with others was probably shaped more by our siblings than by our parents. Some don't like the idea that they were so influenced by their siblings, yet consider what the author of *Mom Loved You Best* says:

The influence of your siblings permeates every aspect of your adult life, from how you make decisions, get along at work with superiors and peers, deal with friends, neighbors, admirers, and enemies, and even how you choose and treat your spouse and raise your children. Your brother(s) or sister(s) shaped you so effectively and indelibly that there is little you can ever do that is not dominated on some level by your relationship with them.

It is their ability to preordain what feels familiar and therefore comfortable to you that gives siblings their greatest and most enduring power over you. In this vast world, the options are infinite. But you will navigate your course everywhere you go guided by your own personal radar system that is programmed to seek out the familiar. Dealing with people and situations you "recognize," however unknowingly, provides a sense of security and control, so you go through life with a tendency to turn everyone you meet into a reincarnation of those you left behind. You will always be attracted to people who resemble your real siblings, whether you were close friends, ardent adversaries, or, more likely, a combination of both. And even when the resemblance isn't all that close, you will see other people as your siblings and so you will involuntarily respond to them as you have always responded to the originals. Most of the time we aren't even aware that we are doing it. And when it is pointed out that we are recreating the familiar, we wonder how we could have been so blind not to see it at the time.[1]

Do you see yourself doing that in your relationships? Reflect on it for a while. And remember, siblings are the ones who give you something you get nowhere else in life.

Let me tell you about two brothers. They were reared in the same family by the same parents. As with many brothers, they were different in various ways. They chose different occupations, and each was successful. But one day a problem arose. One brother experienced an abundance of acceptance and approval. He was the younger of the two. This didn't sit well with the older, since he had a different experience, one that most of us wouldn't like—rejection and disapproval. Who knows if this was the first time something like this had occurred? It could have been, or it could have been a long-standing pattern within their family, as happens in so many. Regardless, this was a turning point in the brothers' lives.

The older brother let the experience seep into the core of his being. He began to seethe with jealousy and resentment. To some extent, sibling rivalry exists in all families, and this could have been what was happening. But it went further than normal sibling rivalry. The two brothers were out together one day, and the older brother killed the younger. Their names were Cain and Abel, the first siblings mentioned in the Bible. Their relationship ended with the death of one at the hands of the other.

The relationships between siblings can be close, loving and supportive, or competitive, tense and unhealthy. Cain couldn't compete with Abel in real life, so he thought he could win over him in another way.

Sibling relationships have always been idealized. They're used as metaphors for the best of human relations. He is "closer than a brother" or she is "like a sister" reflect the ultimate of close ties with others. The "brotherhood of man" is a phrase meant to reflect love and loyalty to the extent that people live together with respect, justice and peace. The term "sisterhood" has been used to reflect feminist strivings of women banding together for a common goal.

Some people have wonderful, fulfilling sibling relationships that epitomize all these terms. Others have lifelong conflicts, although not as intense as the one between Cain and Abel.

I have had counselees express to me statements something like this: "Now that I'm an adult, I thought life would be different. I assumed that I would not have to deal with sibling problems any longer. I don't want to be involved with some of my irritating relatives. In fact, I would be happy never to see some of them again, or at the most, once a year from a distance!"

Resolving Sibling Conflicts

What about you? Have you ever felt like that? Of course, as an adult you can ignore the family members with whom you find it difficult to relate. But there is a price to pay for avoiding relationships, especially with siblings. You may want to evaluate the cost to yourself and others before deciding not to resolve these conflicts.

First, by failing to put to rest issues of sibling conflict, you may experience recurring anger and tension every time you contact that person. Furthermore, your negative feelings usually will spill over onto other family members, complicating the problem.

Second, unresolved conflicts could cause you to dread family get-togethers or reunions for years to come. Many people joyfully anticipate being with their families and spend months planning for these few occasions. But if you have unresolved conflicts, your anticipation of these events is anything but joyful. You're on pins and needles. Your anxiety builds as the date draws near. Then you wear a plastic smile to get through it, while your stomach churns. Is failure to resolve conflicts worth this kind of tension?

Third, there's the guilt. Many today are filled with guilt and regret because they failed to resolve their conflicts with siblings who died unexpectedly. I've talked to many people who said, "If

I had waited another week, it would have been too late." One person told me, "I feel so much better having worked through my relationship with my younger brother to a positive level. I was shocked and saddened when he was killed in an accident, but I knew the air was clear between us, and I have no regrets." Will you be able to say this about your problem relationships?

A fourth major difficulty with choosing to ignore problem relationships, particularly between siblings, is the effect it could have on your own children. Some adults who will not relate to family members deny their children the opportunity to relate to their siblings' families. Restricting a child's relationship with family members may rob him or her of the enjoyment of valuable interaction with aunts, uncles and especially cousins.

Fifth, unresolved family conflicts lead to overreactions and self-fulfilling prophecies. You become supersensitive to the problem sibling to the point that you tend to read false meanings into his or her comments and responses. You may even begin responding negatively to anyone who reminds you of this person, dumping anger and bitterness on unsuspecting and undeserving people.

Finally, unresolved problem relationships put an excessive emotional load on you and you labor under unnecessary anxiety. You know this sibling is a part of your life—whether or not you like it. And you carry inside yourself the image of what the relationship should or could be but is not. The tension between the two creates an emotional burden that will cause you difficulty until the conflicting relationship is resolved.

Ghosts of Sibling Relationships

As you look at your own sibling relationships, the basis for your emotional connection is tied into two elements—age and gender.

These two components are called *access*. Those siblings who are considered high access usually are close in age and the same sex. They spend a lot of time together, sharing experiences and friends. Low access siblings are usually different genders as well as years apart. It's as though they are members of a different generation with their own separate lives. I had a half sister who was 25 years my senior, who seemed more of an acquaintance than a close relative.

The higher the access, the greater the emotional impact—whether good or bad—siblings will have on one another. The more intense the access, the more intense the impact by separation, interference or death.

I've seen those who chose a spouse who reminded them of a brother or sister. You've probably heard the phrase, "Oh, she married her father," but you can marry a sibling just as well, especially when something was left unresolved or unfinished with a particular sibling. Marriage to someone who resembles a sibling may also happen because it creates a comfortable or familiar atmosphere or situation.

Some re-create their brothers or sisters in their choice of friends. If you gave up on a sibling relationship or felt you just had to accept the way your siblings were because you couldn't change them, you may try to create the ideal sibling relationship with a friend. The problem is that you take your patterns of relating with you into new relationships. Instead of creating something new, you create a replication of what existed before. Some call this a repetition compulsion. This can occur in work relationships as it pertains to power. A young sibling in a family may do better taking orders at work than an older sibling who was used to giving them.

Every family has "ghosts." Did you ever think about that? They're called sibling ghosts, and they turn up to haunt you at the

oddest times and strangest places. Scenes from your sibling relationships crop up at different times throughout your adulthood.

Marriage and the selection of a spouse open the sibling
drama. But when your own children arrive it seems that past
scenes are played again. You begin to see your life with your
brothers and sisters reenacted in the gender and birth order of
your own children. For some it's like watching a rerun of your
own family history as you observe your children. And it's not
just a passionless, standoffish observation, but an emotional
connection. You may say, "I see myself in my son. I see my brother in little Jimmy. And, oh, do I feel for my daughter. She needs
so much attention, just like her aunt. I don't know what I feel
about my youngest, though."

You've heard of revivals of plays—when a new production of
a play occurs after it's been out of circulation for many years?
This is similar to what happens in relation to your sibling
memories when your own children are growing up.

> *Thinking about your interaction
> with your siblings may help you
> understand your responses to your children.*

Why is it that a man who was a middle child between two
sisters responds to his own son and two daughters by indulging
his son as he was indulged by his sisters? Or perhaps he encour-
ages his boy to be dependent on his sisters as he was on his own
sisters.

Reenactments can be positive or negative. If you were treated badly by a sibling and you see one of your children in the

image of that sibling, how do you think you may treat that child? Some parents begin identifying their children with their siblings after two or three have arrived, whereas some mothers begin thinking about sibling relationships while still expecting the second child.

Thinking about your interaction with your siblings may help you understand your responses to your children. Sibling patterns in your own life can be repeated with your children. If you tend to overindulge a child, look at your relationships with your siblings. If you tend to favor one child over the other, look back at your siblings. If you tend to reject, look back. If you have mixed feelings, look back. If you dump more on one than the other, look back. Is there a ghost that may be affecting the way you parent your children?

Therapist Selma Fraiberg uses the phrase "ghosts in the nursery" to describe these early sibling relationships that now intrude in your own family. These ghosts usually sneak in unnoticed and say hello to everyone in some of the responses you have to your children.

Ghosts don't stay put in the nursery—not at all. You take them with you everywhere, even to the workplace. Wherever people work there are resemblances to a family environment, whether that environment was healthy or not. Is there someone at work who reminds you of dad or mom, or maybe your brother or sister? Perhaps that person responds and reacts to you as a child or a sibling.

Healthy/Unhealthy Sibling Influences and Interaction

Siblings share genes. They have a genetic glue that binds them together, but it may not mean a true binding of their hearts and minds. As we move through life, interacting with siblings, we don't all experience the same depth of relationship with each one.

Siblings can add so much to life. For instance, they teach one another important social skills. If the family unit is healthy, brothers and sisters create opportunities to learn to get along with others. Siblings learn how to use power, to give and take, to communicate and to get along with someone different from themselves. They learn just how far they can go in dealing with someone and what they can get away with. All of this is preparation for adult life.

But if the family atmosphere is unhealthy, there are problems. If the parents treat the children unequally, the balance is thrown off. A rejected child or one who was not favored by the parents could end up being hard to please, using any means to get attention, including rebellion. A favored child could act snobbish, superior, flaunt the favored position or just become a pain in the neck. These various responses fuel sibling rivalry.

Children in a healthy family form a natural support group. In a healthy family structure, children can respond without involvement on the part of the adults. Siblings may have information and experiences their parents know nothing about. They can support one another against outsiders. If they get along well, they tend to identify with one another's successes and share skills and information with one another. They function as a team rather than separate entities. This can make it easier to function and participate in society later on. But if the family is unhealthy, cooperation may be absent, having been replaced by antagonism and competition. The social skills these siblings fail to learn at home will impact them elsewhere.

Children in a healthy family have their own society of near equals. They learn to relate to someone older or younger. Older children in healthy situations will feel superior to younger children but they won't lord it over them. Younger children realize their position but have a role model to emulate in their older siblings. Younger children gradually follow the progression of the older ones. Without this healthy role model, younger children may have no one near in age to relate to. As a result, they try to behave like adults, even expecting themselves to measure up to adult behavior. This affects their identity, as well as their self-esteem, in a negative way.

In a healthy family, siblings create an atmosphere for growth and learning. They develop skills through their play, learn to use their imaginations and create games. The movie *Wild America*, which showed the adventures of three adolescent brothers, is a classic example. These brothers played tricks on one another but were quick to support and protect each other. The three were adventuresome and creative. They decided to make a homemade movie of endangered species in our country. Their mishaps and near disasters provided entertainment to the viewers, while for these three brothers it provided the beginning of lifetime work and a tremendous contribution to most television viewers around the world. From their adolescent exploits, they eventually became the filmmakers of "Wild Kingdom." Most of the wildlife films we've seen on TV were shot and produced by these brothers.

When children don't have other children as playmates or companions, their only other option may be a parent. Parents tend to impose adult standards on children in unhealthy families. Play and fantasy may be replaced by performance and achievement.

Finally, in a healthy family atmosphere siblings help each other create and maintain an accurate perception of one another as well as of their family. They realize they have much in common. They've shared the same experiences and culture, even though they may have somewhat different perceptions. They use one another's perceptions to help bring their own in line with reality.

But siblings who are intense rivals as children tend to continue the conflict through adulthood. Interactions are either laced with hostility or avoided to diminish the pain. It's not uncommon in these situations to have adult children end up living isolated lives with their own distorted views of family life.

Depleting or Replenishing

One other factor to consider when examining a relationship with a sibling is that, to one degree or another, the relationship is going to be either depleting or replenishing. A depleting relationship is one in which the other person in the relationship drains you emotionally and spiritually. The relationship taps into your energy reserves in some way. Being around this type of person is hard work, an exercise in depletion and coping. And it's not a pretty picture.

Those who deplete you contribute to your problems rather than help you resolve them. If you were to think of yourself as a battery, dealing with these people would leave you without enough juice to get started again!

You don't want a depleting relationship, especially with a sibling. You want replenishment—relationships with people who energize and vitalize you just by being with them. They add to your life in a positive way. Of course, one of the best ways to attract people like this is to be that kind of person yourself.

Siblings have a shared history—games, experiences and secrets that bond them together as adults. Sometimes these memories can fade, particularly if you don't cultivate them. It helps not only to recall what you remember about each sibling but to reflect on your relationship with each one as well. For each of your siblings, answer the following questions. (You may also want to ask your siblings to respond.) Of course, what you do with the response depends upon your relationship.

1. What do you feel were your sibling's positive qualities as a child? What are they now?
2. What do you feel were your sibling's negative qualities as a child? What are they now?
3. How did you feel about this sibling through age 10? From age 11 to 20? From age 21 to 30? At the present time?
4. What emotions did your sibling express openly? How did he/she express them?
5. What was the most pleasant experience you had with this sibling?
6. What was the most unpleasant experience?
7. In what ways are you like your sibling?
8. In what ways are you different from your sibling?
9. In what way has this sibling influenced your life?

As you grow older, it is likely your siblings will become more important to you. Years ago the older generation relied on their children as their primary support system. Today, with so many couples choosing to have only one or two children—or possibly even none—the future for today's young and middle-aged adults will be different. Baby boomers may face their senior years relying not so much on children as on their own brothers and sisters. It appears that more siblings will become the "family glue" for one another. Many may end up living together for economic reasons after they lose their respective spouses. They also may rely upon one another for day-to-day practical support as well as the emotional connection of still belonging to a family unit.

REFLECTING ON YOUR RELATIONSHIPS

It's an adventure to take a look at our sibling relationships. You see the adventure lived out in the sibling stories recorded in the Scriptures—Jacob and Esau, the elder and younger brother in the parable of the prodigal son, Moses and Aaron, Joseph and his older brothers. Perhaps there's something in those relationships that matches your own family experience.

Remember, sibling relationships do not stop at adulthood. They continue, whether in a diminished or intensified capacity, throughout life. They can even be perpetuated at your place of employment or in your own family.

- Your birth order (oldest, middle, youngest child) is a part of your current life. Do you see it?
- Your childhood roles are still with you. Do you know how they still exist?
- Your childhood labels may be gone, but maybe they still affect your perception of yourself.
- Your childhood battles may be over, but now and then they may erupt.
- Your sibling rivalry may still be a part of your life? Can you identify how?

For most adults, their sibling relationships are a mixture of experiences. But what a potential for understanding ourselves and others! As Dr. Jane Greer described it:

[Siblinghood] has the potential for filling our lives with delight, amusement, reassurance and consolation; anger, bafflement, and exasperation; companionship or loneliness; the warmest of friendships or the coldest enmity.[2]

What characterizes your relationships with others? What would you like them to be like? Regardless of your age or circumstances, you can decide what you want, take some risks, make some decisions and implement some changes, all of which can affect the relationships you have with your brothers and sisters, as well as with others. Ultimately, the quality of your relationships shape the very quality of your life.

Notes

1. Drs. William and Madra Hapworth and Joan Rathner Heilman, *Mom Loved You Best* (New York: Viking Penguin, 1993), p. 8.
2. Dr. Jane Greer with Edward Myers, *Adult Sibling Rivalry* (New York: Crown Publishing, 1992), p. 215.

Chapter Two

Your Place in the Family

I'm Jim. I'm the oldest of four children. And I'm the classic firstborn that you read about. I'm responsible, but why shouldn't I be? It was expected of me. I'm an achiever, but why not? That too was expected of me. I'm a caretaker and guardian for my younger siblings, and that should be no surprise. After all—it was expected of me. When I was born, there were no other siblings around home to compete with. When my youngest brother took his first steps and said his first words, the reaction from my parents was, "That's nice." But when I took my first steps, everyone in the neighborhood and at church heard about it, whether they wanted to or not. My parents talked more to me, played with me more and responded to each of my questions with rapt interest and attention. And why not? Unlike the other three, I had no competitors. I had an exclusive contract with Mom and Dad for three years before it was rewritten to make room for my sister. During that time I experienced all sorts of rich emotional responses as well as intellectual challenges. I think my parents would have liked me to have been able to read by age three.

And I did my part. I soon learned what they wanted. I enjoyed all the attention, so I did my best and then some. I talked early, since I was talked to so much. Mom and Dad were my models. I had to learn adult responses as soon as possible. Sometimes I wonder if I'm an overachiever. I do have a tendency to be a workaholic, but I've heard that's not uncommon for us firstborns. I like being in charge, but it was difficult to learn to share my parents with the other three.

Firstborn

If you were the firstborn in your family, perhaps you identify with what you've just read. And if you occupy a second- third- or fourth-born position, Jim may have sounded like your oldest sibling. Although there are plenty of exceptions, there are trends and tendencies for the various birth order positions. Your place in the birth order has shaped who you are today. Your family position not only affected how your parents responded to you but also how much time and attention they could give to you. The order in which you were born came with a set of expectations. Attitudes and skills were shaped, leading to behavior that affected the way you shared, manipulated, controlled, cooperated, conflicted, demanded, helped and supported your family members. And after all the years you spent perfecting these responses, why shouldn't you respond the same way to your own family as well as coworkers?

A firstborn sibling often expects to be in charge. When other children are born, from the very beginning the firstborn feels more capable and superior. This leads firstborns to look at any younger siblings as incapable of reaching their level. Firstborns are comfortable with the power of being first. This feeling usually continues throughout their lives. Parents see them as the enforcers of the family traditions and rules.

In adult life, being a firstborn means seeing yourself as someone to whom others should turn for advice. Often, firstborns see their younger siblings as consulting them even when they aren't. Firstborns feel entitled to have authority in the family and to give advice, solicited or not.

There are some problems, however. There's a tendency for firstborns to take their conscientiousness to an extreme. Firstborns are not the most accepting and tolerant of other viewpoints, and often there is a tendency toward perfectionism.

Firstborns may seem more conservative in contrast to their siblings, but a second- or last-born may be more creative and willing to take risks. Firstborns usually follow through and finish what they start, so their parents not only rely upon them but also perhaps put too much responsibility on them.

UNDER THE MICROSCOPE

One of the other pressures placed upon firstborns by parents is the belief that extended family and friends are waiting to see how the first child responds, then they will make their assessment on how the family is doing. Firstborns sense that they're under the microscope. This is detrimental if it makes them search for external validation to believe they're all right. Grandparents often contribute to this problem if they dote on the child. There isn't any other child in the system who has to deal with performance ratings as much as a firstborn.

Lest the picture is painted that all firstborns are overachievers, remember there are many who are or at least feel they are underachievers. If expectations are too high, discouragement sets in, and they may give up in some ways.[1]

> *There isn't any other child in the family system who has to deal with performance ratings as much as a firstborn.*

Sometimes younger siblings refer to the firstborn as the "little mom" or "little dad." And it's as true now as it has been for thousands of years. A firstborn son is a prized possession and has the first opportunity to claim the fruits of his parents' success. Firstborns also are more apt to experience everything new, such as clothes, stroller, car seat, crib, trike, whereas the others may end up using previously owned materials.

RESPONSIBLE—AND RESENTFUL

In the story of the forgiving father in Luke 15, we have an older-son scenario. When he heard that his younger prodigal brother had returned home and his father was celebrating, he reacted like this:

> The older brother stalked off in an angry sulk and refused to join in. His father came out and tried to talk to him, but he wouldn't listen. The son said, "Look how many years I've stayed here serving you, never giving you one moment of grief, but have you ever thrown a party for me and my friends? Then this son of yours who has

thrown away your money on whores shows up and you go all out with a feast!" (Luke 15:28-30, *THE MESSAGE*).

We have a self-righteous, overly responsible brother, attempting to maintain his own sense of adequacy while trying to please his father. He was so caught up in this that he failed to see his father's gracious heart. He was so full of pride that it led to judgment. He was angry, resentful, full of rules that he probably couldn't even keep himself. He was sorry to see his brother return; in fact, he probably was happy to see him leave in the first place. After all, it restored him to being the only son at home. Perhaps he thought he wouldn't have to share his parents with his brother ever again. But he was wrong. His brother, even though in a distant land, was always on his father's heart and mind. Not only that, but when you've been the only one for several years, you feel entitled to remain playing the lead role in the family drama. Another side to this, however, is that many younger siblings don't experience the same strictness as firstborns. They may have more latitude all the way through life, leaving an elder sibling to wonder why.

As we consider the relationship between the younger and elder brother in this story, perhaps the elder and his concerns became lost in the focus on the younger son and the father. The younger came back with a confession that would elicit a response from his father. He came home after spending all of his inheritance, which was no small amount. It wasn't anything he had earned, yet his father pulled out all the stops: new clothes, new jewelry, the best calf for a barbecue and a party. There is nothing said of punishment, lectures, restrictions or earning of trust. And the celebration started before the elder brother even arrived home. He heard the music and dancing, smelled the food and probably said, "What's this?" He felt slighted. After all, he was faithful and diligent. Why wasn't that recognized? Many have been through this experience.

Barbara Brown Taylor describes something similar in her own life:

> I am an eldest child myself. I know what it is like to break in parents, to step aside as they exercise their new and improved skills on younger siblings, and then to take the rap for the little criminals when they mess up. I remember one Saturday afternoon when I was supposed to be looking after my two sisters and my parents came home early. Within minutes they had hauled me by my elbows to the upstairs bathroom to show me my little sister clutching a fat black crayon in her fist, putting the finishing touches on the claw-footed porcelain bathtub that had once been white. Did she get spanked? No, she was just a little baby who did not know any better. Yes, I was the older sister who should have kept her out of trouble.[2]

Older siblings frequently get the raw end of the deal, as the elder brother apparently does in the parable at hand. My guess is that he was not as incensed by his younger brother's return or his father's forgiveness of him as he was by the celebration.

GUINEA PIGS AND PERFORMING PONIES

The older brother had a point. Firstborns may be the center of their parents' attention, but they are receiving the care and attention of inexperienced amateurs. Yes, firstborns have a time of exclusivity with their parents, but they also end up being an experiment of sorts, because parents' first efforts are centered on firstborns. Often, a firstborn girl is expected to be "Mother's helper," which can include being a baby-sitter, disciplinarian and cleaning woman. It's not surprising that some firstborn women of large families have opted not to have children of their own; they feel they've raised a family already.

Some are expected to carry on family values and traditions. Firstborns can end up with incredible stress as they try to live up to the expectations of the parents. And they never get away from the responsibility. Barbara Sullivan describes it in this way:

> Why is it that so many parents give the lion's share of responsibility to their oldest children? Is it only because they are the oldest, or is it something inherent in the character of firstborns?
>
> A responsible individual, according to Edith Neisser, is one who is concerned with the needs and welfare of others. "Those who are responsible," she says, "tend to be those who are also somewhat conscientious, conforming and competent. These qualities are prominent in many first children."[3]

Some firstborns end up feeling that what counts in life is performance, not relationships. Some are resentful, not over the responsibilities, but over the lack of privileges.[4] This is why many end up feeling they are responsible for the relationships in the family. Some also have a hard time asking for help or depending on others, because they're used to making decisions and being on center stage.

Firstborns also have to deal with statements like "You're older; you should know better"; "You have to set a good example for the others"; "You know, we do expect more from you." As parents age, firstborns may end up being the ones to look after their health, finances and possible living placement.

PARADISE LOST

At some point in time, the firstborn's world collapses. Trouble is on the horizon for nine months. Dethronement is not an easy process. It's a loss for most children, no matter how well parents plan. It's an easier transition if the parents take care to see that the first child's emotional needs are met and they handle the jealousy well, enabling the child to understand that he or she is still loved.

At a seminar on crisis and loss, I asked the participants to reflect back and identify the first loss they could remember as a child. A woman in her fifties raised her hand and said, "My first loss came when my younger sister was born. I was dethroned." And right next to her sat her younger sister with a smile on her face.

It's not uncommon for a firstborn to give up and regress to infancy. It's the child's way of getting attention.[5] After the second child is born, there is less sensitivity to the first child's needs; the firstborn usually has to begin taking the initiative to play or talk with mom.

Middle Children

If you weren't a firstborn, you may have been the intruder—the second-born child. There are benefits to being the second child born. A second-born is the beneficiary to a less intensive list of expectations from the now experienced and more relaxed parents. The parents may even be more indulgent and tolerant of shortcomings. Because they expect less, they may enjoy this child more.

Most second children are well acquainted with the phrase "hand-me-downs." I've seen various responses to this. With two boys close in age, there was resentment on the part of the younger; two other brothers, who were nine years apart, didn't seem to have this problem because of hero worship on the part of the younger, who enjoyed receiving anything from his older brother.

What do second-borns tend to be like? Are they replicas of their siblings, or are they totally opposite? Either can be true, but many tend to be just the opposite. They may develop characteristics their older sibling lacks. They're not concerned with parental approval. They don't have as much to lose and may be more experimental. Often they vacillate between roles until they find one they like. If they are a middle child and the oldest of their sex, they tend to share the characteristics of both a middle child and firstborn. But if they are a middle child of the same sex as the oldest, they tend to take on the qualities found in the youngest sibling.

SANDWICH FIXIN'S

If the second-born is a middle child, he ends up in somewhat of a double bind. He knows what it's like to feel inferior (to the oldest) but also what it's like to feel superior (to the next born). He may feel squeezed on both sides. His older sibling wants to stay on the throne and rule over everyone, but the third or younger child wants to climb over the second, dethrone him and move up. (How might this position replay itself at work or in a marriage? Consider what might happen if a second-born marries a firstborn or a third-born.)

One middle child said, "Do you know what it's like to feel like a displaced person or an immigrant whose papers have been lost? That was me. Sometimes I didn't know where I belonged. My older sister could do more and do it better, and then my younger sibling knew how to get attention. It was like going to the store, taking a number and waiting for your number to be called. I just wanted some attention. The others didn't have to work so hard to get what they needed. Sometimes I felt like the middle of a sandwich."

Some feel that second-borns (middle-borns) end up having difficulty making decisions. Caution is their middle name. They may get all the facts, but they procrastinate. It's more comfortable for others to bail them out by making decisions for them. If forced to decide, they may toss out all the research they've done and go on impulse. They're not as gifted or equipped as first-borns to be decisive, nor as adept at risk-taking as the third-born (youngest). Middle children tend to second-guess themselves. When they do decide, they analyze their decision to death: "Was that the right decision? What if it doesn't work out?" That's why second-borns find it easier to lean on others' decisive qualities and just go with the flow.

At the same time, middle children often have the positive quality of knowing how to give and take. They possess a flexibility that works well for them in getting along with others. They learned from their siblings how to play one off against the other.[6]

There are definite benefits to being the second-born. Second-borns can reap the benefits of the pioneering effort of the firstborn. Mistakes can be avoided, and when the oldest begins to move out of the family system in adolescence, the second-born can move up to that coveted position to rule over younger siblings.[7]

Second or middle children start their lives not just with parents but with a peer, one who can be a companion as well as a rival. It's a mixed blessing, for the one they like they also can hate at times. The older sibling has mixed feelings, too.

Second-borns have the potential of being mentored by their older sibling. They can imitate that sibling and benefit from his or her trial-and-error experiences with parents. If the oldest sibling is much older than the second-born, the second child may end up feeling as if he or she has three parents instead of just two, since there are three people giving orders. And if second-borns are also middle children, throughout their lives they are often referred to as "John's little brother" and "Susan's big brother."[8]

A friend of mine who is in his fifties is a second-born child. He once took a vacation with a friend and his older sister and her husband, all of whom were firstborns. He told about his frustration of being bossed around and treated like a younger sibling for three days. "There we were, four adults, and yet they still didn't see me as being on their level."

The Youngest

When you hear the words "last born" or "youngest," what images come to mind? Do you think of "the clown," "the spoiled one," "the favorite," "the pest," "the one who got away with murder"?

LOVED IN LITERATURE

Just as with the other birth positions, we have images and stereotypes about the last-born or youngest. In myths, folklore and fairy tales, the youngest usually comes out on top. In 20 percent of Grimm's fairy tales, there are three children. Yet the first and second child came out on top only 8 percent of the time, while the third- (or last-) born won 52 percent of the time. It doesn't seem fair, does it? And winning in these stories meant they were able to triumph over the meanness, selfishness and even treachery of the older siblings.

An example of this is seen in the story "The Queen Bee." The youngest son, Simpleton, is sent out by his father to find his immoral and shameless brothers. He does so, and on the way home he's seen to be resourceful and kind, although his older brothers don't think much of him. His brothers want to kill some animals, but Simpleton saves them. Later, the grateful animals help him when he has to overcome some difficult tasks. One of the creatures he saves was the queen of the beehive. She in turn helps him select the most beautiful of three seemingly identical princesses. As a bonus, the one he selects just happens to be the favored youngest sister. And, of course, the two marry, and Simpleton inherits her kingdom.

Why is it that so many stories handed down from generation to generation favor the last-born child? Some say that younger children who may have felt they were low man on the totem pole were able to reflect their dilemma in these tales and create, in fantasy, a fulfillment of their dream to come out on top. Others believe these reflect reality, that the youngest really do have a favored position and get more of the breaks. Perhaps there really are some benefits in being the youngest.[9]

It's interesting to see the interaction between younger siblings and the firstborn in the Scriptures. Isaac came out better than his older brother, Ishmael. Jacob took both the blessing and the birthright from his firstborn twin, Esau. Rachel gained Jacob's love and retained it, but her older sister, Leah, was not Jacob's favorite.

However, when Jacob fell in love with Rachel and not her older sister, Leah, he created a problem. Their father, Laban, decided to take care of the problem, so he replaced Rachel with Leah in the bridal chamber. His response when he was confronted by Jacob is perhaps an age-old policy: "It is not the practice in our place, to marry off the younger before the first-born" (Gen. 29:26, *NASB*). What was the result? Competition for years over who could produce the most children.

Joseph, off to a shaky start in life, ended up doing much better than his brothers. Moses, rather than his older brother, Aaron, led the people out of Israel.

Dr. Peter Neubauer had an interesting thought. He said it appears that firstborns have privileges given to them by their birth order; all others have to earn their privileges.[10]

Youngest children have special positions in the family that no one else will ever experience. They will never be dethroned like their older siblings. There's no new kid on the horizon. They never have to look over their shoulder. They can bypass the developmental attainments of their older siblings since they have good examples to learn from and follow. And by now the parents are probably more relaxed and permissive. This is especially true when the last-born is the first girl or boy in the family. Because last-borns are the babies of the family, they may never be the recipient of more attention and favor, but they'll never have to relinquish the exclusive parent-child bond. All the major players are in place.

STRUGGLING WITH INSECURITIES

There's also a downside to being the youngest. Many end up being known as the baby of the family all their lives. Perhaps they were overpowered by everyone else, which made it difficult to be recognized as adults in their own right. If older siblings controlled them while at home, they'll probably continue this pattern into adulthood. The oldest siblings may take care of the youngest and make excuses for them, even as adults. It's easy for the youngest children to feel less important, less competent and less independent because they came last. One last-born told me, "I don't feel a part of the family circle. I get my strokes and identity outside, from others."

Resentment and dependency are common reactions in last-borns. They may work very hard to catch up to the others, which can be a positive thing. But some overextend themselves by taking on projects, problems and involvements that are too much for them. When things don't work out, it heightens their feelings of dependency, inferiority and frustration.

When you're the last-born, it's quite easy to spend your life looking for others to take the initiative and lead. The others are already out there in front; this, combined with lesser expectations for last-borns, is fertile ground for creating this sort of dependent lifestyle. Some feel insecure about their efforts and abilities because they have been compared with the older siblings' accomplishments. The last-borns may want to be out in the lead but aren't sure they can handle it.

Other last-borns look forward to the time when they are adults and can be freed from the fetters and bondage of family position, and break out in front. But it doesn't often happen that way. The patterns and responses to others are too deeply ingrained. Why would the fears that accompanied you in childhood suddenly disappear once the older siblings are gone and you're on your own? The youngest are more likely than others to be dependent. After all, if others are always around, willing and able to do things for them, there's no need to learn how to do them—or at least that's how many last-borns may think.

Even though last-borns may appear helpless and dependent, they do exert control over others by their cooperation in being served. After all, if someone is always doing something for you and serving you, who ends up being the servant? It's certainly not the last-born. Consider this: What happens in a marriage if a youngest son marries an oldest daughter?

When others do a lot for you and your efforts never compare with the others, do you grow up feeling secure, competent and ready to face the world? You may end up discouraged, feeling everyone else is better than you, so your efforts at direct competition may not be the best. Subtle doubt may accompany proficient, successful last-borns throughout their adult lives.

Youngest children can be very perceptive, observant and creative, since they've learned what works and what doesn't from watching the others and gaining insights from their experiences. Who else gets this opportunity?

The youngest is often the "rule changer." The author of *Mom Loved You Best* says:

> They will test the limits and try to see what they can get away with. They are often the siblings who are the most radical, the most rebellious, the most likely to accept new theories, and the least likely to relate to authority figures. They are the ones who develop new routes, new ways to reach their goals. They can't play by the rules because early on they lacked the equipment with which to compete. If the goal was to see who could run the fastest or write the best or win the contest, they didn't stand a chance. So they interrupted the game by getting sick or hurt—or they changed the rules to suit themselves.
>
> The babies of the family often receive extra doses of affection and attention and, in the eyes of their siblings, are often allowed to "get away with murder" by parents who tend to become more permissive with each child. They are likely to be fun-loving, charming, affectionate, and coy, people who have learned how to get their own way by cajoling and wheedling.[11]

Because youngest children seem to buck the system, some become discouraged, while others find new ways to do things.

Sometimes last-borns wonder where they fit in, based on receiving minimal attention from parents. No one is really that worked up over their arrival.

Author Kevin Leman, himself a classic last-born, gives another insight into this position:

> Youngest children in the family are typically the outgoing charmers, the personable manipulators. They are also affectionate, uncomplicated, and sometimes a little absentminded. Their "space cadet" approach to life gets laughs, smiles, and shakes of the head. Last borns are the most likely to show up at the elementary school's "sing" or the Sunday school picnic unzipped or unbuttoned in some delicately obvious area. Without doubt, they can be a little different.
>
> It stands to reason then that the family clown or entertainer is likely to be the last born. Nobody told me that—I just naturally assumed the role. I was the Dennis the Menace type. What I wanted was attention. That was my thing in life—getting people to laugh or point or comment.
>
> There were at least two good reasons for my thirst to achieve "stardom": a brother five years older who was 9.75 in everything, and a sister eight years older who was a perfect 10.00. Ever since I could remember it seemed that I scored around 1.8 in comparison to their abilities and achievements.
>
> A typical characteristic of the last born is that he is more carefree and vivacious—a real "people person" who is usually popular in spite of (because of?) his clowning antics.
>
> Get the family together for the big Thanksgiving or Christmas photo. Work tenaciously to maneuver every-

one into the place and to snap the shutter when everyone looks halfway sane and—whoops! Who's that over on the left with the crossed eyes, trying to touch his nose with his tongue? Yes, it's last-born Buford (who in this picture may be twenty-six years old) doing his thing for a laugh.

Or maybe Buford is doing his thing for other reasons. There is another mainstream of qualities in most last borns. Besides being charming, outgoing, affectionate, and uncomplicated, they can also be rebellious, critical, temperamental, spoiled, impatient, and impetuous.[12]

These coping patterns, whether positive or negative, whether firstborn or last, are set incredibly early in life. In the book *Breaking Points,* the story of John Hinckley Jr., the young man who attempted to assassinate President Reagan, is presented. The story tells how John was born two days before the new hospital opened in the town of Ardmore, Texas. Because of this, when he was transferred to the new hospital after it opened, he had to be kept in a room all by himself because of his exposure to the outside world. His mother, Jo Ann, in remembering the incident, felt this was symbolic: "Alone . . . separated from his peers . . . years later was to become John's pattern."[13]

An article written in the *Chicago Tribune* magazine section talks about a woman bodybuilder named Jo Wood. She was the third and youngest of three girls. Her mother and father were achievers, and her two older sisters both had multiple advanced degrees. In her own words, her two older sisters "knew where they were going. From adolescence on, they did everything right." Jo described herself this way: "I was a little misfit." She drifted aimlessly through school and several colleges, "still in search of everything her family had found years before." Then one day she walked into the school weight room and realized she could become the strongest woman in the world. This was the turning point. At that moment Jo Wood found her identity, as unusual as it might seem to most women. Since that time she has put her life in danger through the misuse of drugs and severe training techniques. From all appearances, this quest dominates and consumes her life. She is willing to risk everything to keep her sense of identity; the pain of training is nothing compared to the pain of isolation.[14]

In a sense, youngest children are forced to be creative, and they usually don't mind being a bit different. How this reads out in their lives, however, can take many directions.[15]

The Scriptures give a unique illustration of three siblings in the book of Hosea. Hosea, a prophet of God, was committed to marry Gomer, an unfaithful wife, and to conceive children with her. This was to symbolize the unfaithfulness of the children of Israel "in departing from the Lord" (1:2). Each of the three children born to Gomer and Hosea was given a symbolic name. It's interesting to note the accuracy of the symbolism in the lives of the first three children. In the first chapter of Hosea, the first child born was a son:

> Then the Lord said to Hosea, "Call him Jezreel, because I will soon punish the house of Jehu for the massacre at Jezreel, and I will put an end to the kingdom of Israel" (v. 4).

The Expositor's Bible Commentary says, "The use of the name Jezreel here looks *back to the time and also ahead to the future day*, when 'the blood' Jehu then shed would be avenged, as the next words indicate" (emphasis added). This is the very characteristic of the first child: "He had two faces—one is turned to his parents who represent the past; the other looks on to his brothers and sisters, thereby gazing into the future."[16]

Hosea's second child was a daughter. "Then the Lord said to Hosea, 'Call her Lo-Ruhamah, for I will no longer show love to the house of Israel, that I should at all forgive them'" (v. 6). Her name means, literally, "not loved." One of the struggles of the second child is often rejection—a feeling of not being loved.

Gomer also had a third child, a son. "Then the Lord said, 'Call him Lo-Ammi, for you are not my people, and I am not your God'" (v. 9). The name Lo-Ammi is harsher in meaning than the name of the second child. The name Lo-Ruhamah spoke of not being loved; Lo-Ammi speaks of being fully disowned. Many third (youngest) children feel disowned from their family, wondering where they fit in.[17]

So where are you in all of this? If you're a first-, second- or third-born, did you fit the descriptions?

Of course, these are generalized descriptions. There are always variations and exceptions. But it's also quite normal to fit the classic descriptions. Upon understanding their birth order, a number of people have said, "It's good to know that what I went through and how I felt growing up was normal. I don't feel so odd now."

Effects of Birth Order in Other Relationships

How does your birth order affect how you relate at work? Have you ever asked your coworkers their birth order? Is there any "sibling" rivalry going on at work? Is there a favorite or a scapegoat? Remember, if you view some of your coworkers as siblings, you won't respond to them in a dispassionate, neutral way. You will respond with feeling. Have you ever wondered why you're fearful of one, resentful of another, doting toward someone else and ambivalent to another? Could it be that your feelings toward these people have some correlation with your feelings toward your siblings?

If you're a firstborn, whom do you see and respond to at work as younger siblings? If you're a second-, middle- or last-born, whom do you see and respond to at work as older siblings? Remember Mr. Spock in "Star Trek"? Leonard Nimoy played this part. He was nominated for an Emmy as best-supporting actor, even though this was a star role. He actually preferred this because he'd been taught as a second son not to upstage his older brother. He was much more comfortable with a supporting role; had he been a firstborn, he might have felt differently.

Some companies' human resource divisions report that women with several sisters at home do well because they're adept at cooperating and negotiating on the job.

Look at your close friendships. What are their birth orders in their families of origin? Is the pattern of the past playing out with your friends? Why is it that some have one or two close friends, while others have four or five? Does this reflect their family patterns? Could it have something to do with the numbers in their family or the degree of closeness that existed there?[18] Who attracts you? Who repels you?

As children become adolescents and then adults, there's a process occurring in their lives that affects their mate selection. Most aren't even aware of this force guiding or drawing them on. In looking for a lifelong partner, you're looking for someone who seems to "fit" with you. The degree of fit you feel with different people is no accident. It's based in part on gender and in part on birth order, complementarily. For example, if you are a man and the oldest in the family, with a younger sister, who might you fit with best? Would it be a woman who was the oldest sister of sisters or the youngest who had older brothers? The oldest sister is gender compatible. You do know something about females younger than you. But a firstborn woman? You don't know that much about this one; also, two firstborns have a great potential for control and conflict issues. Add to this the fact that an oldest sister of sisters is lacking in experience with brothers, especially a firstborn man.

Who are you married to? Have you and your spouse discussed the impact of your birth order on the way you relate to one another?

Thinking It Through

What is your life like now? If you're a firstborn, are you responding as a firstborn to everyone else in your life? If so, how is it working? If you're a second- third- or last-born, are you responding to everyone else in your life accordingly? If so, is it working? Do you wonder why other people respond to you the way they do? How are your relationships working out?

> *Once it dawns on you how your sibling interactions are being replicated in your life, it's time to decide if that's the way you want to continue to respond.*

When you talk to your siblings today, is it similar to your childhood interaction? When you all get together, is it like entering a time machine and returning to scenes from your childhood, or have all of you changed and adapted?

Once it dawns on you how your sibling interactions are being replicated in your life, then it's time to decide if that's the way you want to continue to respond. No one has to remain stuck in childhood behavior patterns.

Kevin Leman, in *The Birth Order Book*, provides an excellent summation of all we have discussed in this chapter—both the challenges and the realities of being a first-, second- or last-born sibling. He says,

1. As important as a child's order of birth may be, it is only an influence, not a final fact of life forever set in cement and unchangeable as far as how that child will turn out.
2. The way parents treat their children is equally important to their birth order, environment, physical and mental characteristics.
3. Every birth order has inherent strengths and weaknesses. Parents must accept both while helping the child develop positive traits and cope with negative ones.
4. No birth order is better or more desirable than another. Firstborns seem to have a corner on achievement and the headlines, but the door is wide open for later borns to make their mark. It is up to them.
5. Birth order information does not give the total psychological picture for anyone. No system of personality development can do that. Birth order statistics and characteristics are indicators that combine with physical, mental, and emotional factors to give the bigger picture.
6. Understanding some basic principles of birth order is not a formula for automatically solving problems or changing your personality overnight. Changing oneself is the hardest task any human being can attempt; it takes long, hard work.[19]

Notes

1. Margaret M. Hooper, Ph.D., and James M. Harper, Ph.D., *Birth Order Roles and Sibling Patterns in Individual and Family Therapy* (Rockville, Md.: Asten, 1987), pp. 35-38, adapted.
2. Barbara Brown Taylor, *Christianity Today*, 26 October 1998, p. 72.
3. Barbara Sullivan and Karl Konig, *Brothers and Sisters* (Blaurvelt, New York: St. George Books, 1963), pp. 46, 47.
4. Ibid., pp. 52, 53, adapted.
5. Helene S. Arnstein, *Brothers and Sisters/Sisters and Brothers* (New York: E.P. Dutton, 1979), pp. 97,98, adapted.
6. Drs. William and Madra Hapworth and Joan Rathner Heilman, *Mom Loved You Best* (New York: Viking Penguin, 1993), pp. 62-66, adapted.
7. Arnstein, *Brothers/Sisters*, p. 110, adapted.
8. Dr. Jane Greer with Edward Myers, *Adult Sibling Rivalry* (New York: Crown Publishing, 1992), p. 25, adapted.
9. Arnstein, *Brothers/Sisters*, pp. 119, 120, adapted.
10. Francine Klagsbrun, *Mixed Feelings* (New York: Bantam Books, 1992), p. 64, adapted.
11. Hapworth and Heilman, *Mom*, pp. 60, 61.
12. Dr. Kevin Leman, *The Birth Order Book* (Old Tappan, N. J.: Fleming H. Revell, 1984), pp. 82-84. Printed by permission.
13. Sullivan and Konig, *Brothers and Sisters*, p. 137, adapted.
14. Ibid., p. 141, adapted.
15. Hapworth and Heilman, *Mom*, pp. 58-61. See also Patti McDermott, *Sisters and Brothers* (Los Angeles: Lowell House, 1992), pp. 43-52; Greer and Myers, *Adult Sibling Rivalry*, p. 26.
16. Frank E. Gaebelein, *The Expositor's Bible Commentary*, Vol. 7 (Grand Rapids, Mich.: Regency Reference Library of the Zondervan Publishing House, 1985), pp. 171, 172.
17. Sullivan and Konig, *Brothers and Sisters*, p. 142, adapted.
18. Klagsbrun, *Mixed*, pp. 338-50, adapted.
19. Leman, *Birth Order*, p. 182. Printed by permission.

Chapter Three

Favorites in Your Family?

While growing up, you may have heard some statements like this: "Mom always liked you best"; "Dad always cut you more slack." Perhaps you said those words at some time in your life. When this happens in a family, the unequal love from a parent can dominate two areas of a child's life—feelings about self and his or her relationship with siblings. When a child feels like the outcast, his emotional life can be dominated by what he hasn't received, what he has missed, and the urgent desire to make up for those losses.

The pain experienced is the pain of rejection, the feeling of being thought less of in the parents' eyes. If this happened to you, no matter what you do or how hard you try, there is an internal ache that won't go away. It affects the way you respond to others in adolescence and as an adult. Some of us carry a fear or expectation of rejection throughout our lives.

A Classic Case Study

Joseph was a favored youngest son but a hated brother. He was the son of Jacob, an older but passive father. To understand the family dynamics, we need to note how Jacob responded to other events in his life:

> Now Dinah the daughter of Leah, whom she had borne to Jacob, went out to visit the daughters of the land. And when Shechem the son of Hamor the Hivite, the prince of the land, saw her, he took her and lay with her by force (Gen. 34:1,2, *NASB*).

When Dinah's father, Jacob, heard about this, he did nothing. Her brothers did, however. They devised a plan, deceived the Hivites who fell into their trap, and killed all the men in the city. They then proceeded to carry off all the wealth, women and children (see v. 29).

Jacob was upset and angry over what his sons had done. But what concerned him was his reputation with the rest of the people in the land.

Another family crisis occurred not long after:

> Then Israel [Jacob] journeyed on and pitched his tent beyond the tower of Eder. And it came about while Israel was dwelling in that land, that Reuben went and lay with Bilhah his father's concubine; and Israel heard of it (35:21,22, *NASB*).

Jacob's son Reuben had sexual relations with Bilhah, who was the mother of two of Reuben's half brothers. Did Jacob do anything when he heard about it? Not at all.

SIBLINGS AND SOAP OPERA SCENARIOS

Joseph was born into a home filled with siblings; it also was filled with deception, intrigue, anger, rebellion, rivalry and out-of-control jealousy.

From the time Joseph was born, he was the favorite. He was a child of Jacob's old age. And it seemed that his character was different from that of his brothers. It could be that's why Jacob favored him. Unfortunately, Jacob showed Joseph great favoritism, which sent a message to the other siblings. The brothers soon realized that Joseph was his father's pet, which didn't surprise them too much, since Joseph's mother was Jacob's favorite wife. On top of that, Jacob did something that incensed the older brothers:

> Now Israel [Jacob] loved Joseph more than all his sons, because he was the son of his old age; and he made him a varicolored tunic (37:3, *NASB*).

Jacob had eleven sons who were hard to raise, and now he had one who was easy to handle. Remember, a passive father, particularly an older one, tends to favor the child who isn't difficult; and Jacob was blatant about his favoritism!

ONE SAW MANY COLORS; ELEVEN SAW RED!

There was more to it than meets the eye. Scholars generally think this garment was long-sleeved and extended all the way to the ankles. You can't work very well in this kind of a coat. It's a costly coat, a nonfunctional coat. It's a coat that sends a message. In Joseph's time you didn't go to work in the fields dressed like this. You wore a short, sleeveless tunic. By giving this coat, which was also a sign of nobility, Jacob sent a message: "Joseph can wear this outfit because he doesn't have to work like the rest of you." No wonder there was so much unrest. The brothers weren't blind:

> And his brothers saw that their father loved him more than all his brothers; and so they hated him and could not speak to him on friendly terms (37:4, *NASB*).

Jealousy and hostility were so intense that any remarks made to Joseph probably were laced with sarcasm and verbal jabs. But the brothers also were angry at him for another reason:

> Joseph, when seventeen years of age, was pasturing the flock with his brothers while he was still a youth. . . . And Joseph brought back a bad report about them to their father (v. 2, *NASB*).

Joseph made sure his brothers were seen in a bad light. We don't know whether they deserved it or not. From what we know about them, they probably did. There was a high level of competition between the brothers. There usually is, as compared with sisters.

FUEL FOR THE FIRES OF JEALOUSY

Joseph knew his position with his father. He probably believed he was a cut above his brothers, so he continued to add insult to injury. He rubbed it in. He wasn't an easy brother to love or to be around. When he told his brother about his dreams, it was the last straw:

> Joseph had a dream, and when he told it to his brothers, they hated him more. He said to them, "Listen to this dream I had: We were binding sheaves of grain out in the field when suddenly my sheaf rose and stood upright, while your sheaves gathered around mine and bowed down to it."
>
> His brothers said to him, "Do you intend to reign over us? Will you actually rule us?" And they hated him all the more because of his dream and what he had said (vv. 5-8).

His brothers were seething with anger. If he didn't know it, he was blind. If he did know it, then he must have had a death wish, because he turned right around and shared his next dream with them:

> Then he had another dream, and he told it to his brothers. "Listen," he said, "I had another dream, and this time the sun and moon and eleven stars were bowing down to me."
>
> When he told his father as well as his brothers, his father rebuked him and said, "What is this dream that you had? Will your mother and I and your brothers actually come and bow down to the ground before you?" His brothers were jealous of him, but his father kept the matter in mind (vv. 9-11).

This was the crowning blow. Later, while the brothers were out taking care of the flocks, Jacob sent Joseph out to check on them. Wasn't this father aware of his older sons' hatred and jealousy? Was he blind? When the brothers saw Joseph coming, they began plotting against him. Yet, even with this opportunity in front of them, they couldn't bring themselves to kill him. They just wanted him gone. So they decided that selling him into slavery in Egypt was a convenient solution.

Some favorite children can't be dismissed that easily. They don't or won't go away. They continue to remind the other siblings, in actions and sometimes in words, who they are. Joseph had to remind his brothers of his identity when he came face to face with them years later: "I am your brother Joseph, whom you sold into Egypt" (45:4, *NASB*).

Joseph, Yes; Josephine, No

I've seen rejection and favoritism occur just because the baby wasn't the right sex! Some parents have their hearts set so strongly upon having either a boy or girl that when they discover their hopes will not, or have not, been fulfilled, their response of love and acceptance is dulled. Have you ever heard someone say, "Isn't that wonderful? Their first child was a boy! Now the family name can be carried on. They can have all the girls they want." I wonder how Jacob would have responded to his last-born if the child's name had been Josephine rather than Joseph!

Who doesn't want a son? Every parent does. In the Old Testament we hear Rachel crying out to her husband, Jacob, to give her sons, "or I'll die" (Gen. 30:1). Girls sometimes wonder why their brothers were given special treatment. There's a reason. Most cultures value sons over daughters. If you lived in Old Testament times, and even into the early centuries, you would have seen that it was the firstborn son who received the inheritance.

Consider this trend in various cultures. The eldest son in Asian families has such a position of high respect that at an early age the younger siblings learn to defer to him without question.

In China, Korea and India, the preference for sons is so extreme that a child is aborted if fetal tests show that it's a girl. In these countries, when food is scarce, more will be given to the sons than to the daughters. In Greek culture, a mother gains prestige when she has a son. This son's sisters are raised with the understanding that they must be obedient to him.

Sons still are given preference in numerous ways in our country, in spite of the emphasis of the women's movement. A son can carry on the family name and line. For some fathers, a son gives them a second chance for what they never attained. They relive their hopes and aspirations through their sons.

At the height of her acting career, Barbara Sullivan said in an interview that her father was so angry and disappointed when she was born—a third daughter instead of another son—that he left home in anger and didn't return for hours. She described her experience of rejection in this way:

> On the occasion of my parents' fiftieth wedding anniversary, my father had a large celebration dinner. While we were at the door waiting to welcome the guests, I was standing between my father and my older brother, Tom. As the first couple entered the room, Dad greeted them and then reached in front of me to put his arm around my brother. "And this is our son, Tom," he said proudly.
>
> As I stood between them, I seemed for a moment to be suspended outside of time. At last I could see objectively what my subconscious mind had known all my life; my dad (and also my mother) preferred boys. This realization aroused no anger or resentment, but rather a sort of "eureka!" feeling that so many things had finally come into focus.
>
> My parents never consciously showed a preference for my brother—and they were, in fact, pleased that their second child was a girl. Like many others in our society, however, they held some basic belief that males have greater value than females. Some Christian teaching seems to propagate the theory that even God prefers men over women. This belief manifested itself in many areas, including that of education.[1]

John McDermott, the author of *Raising Cain (and Abel, Too)*, says:

> Nothing is more potentially serious for distorting personality development (as well as complicating and intensifying sibling rivalry) than parents preferring one sex

over the other. The child of the "wrong" gender will feel disappointed in his or her sex, whichever it is.[2]

While clearly defining the roles of men and women, the Scriptures also state, "In the Lord . . . woman is not independent of man, nor is man independent of woman" (1 Cor. 11:11). There may be a difference in roles but not in value.

Other Reasons for Parental Favoritism or Rejection

Parents rejecting a child is by no means an uncommon occurrence in our society, nor is the favoring of one child over another. There are numerous reasons for this.

One reason is that parents may find it easy to connect with one child but not another. Whether it be looks or personality, the parents just don't care for the child. Some children are rejected because of an apparent defect, such as a low IQ or because another child in the family is more attractive or gifted. In some cases, if a child too closely mirrors the image of a parent with self-hate, it is easy for that parent to project those feelings of dislike onto the child. Children who resemble the other side of the family may receive the fallout of stored-up hostility. This anger may be directed against the spouse or even against the spouse's parents yet be projected onto the child. Or if a child is the result of an untimely pregnancy, there may be a sense of rejection. Often a "surprise child" later in life is seen as an interference. (Unfortunately, some parents have a child not because they want one, but because they don't know how not to have one.) And of course, some parents want to have a child of a certain sex, and they reject the child who is born the wrong gender.

Sometimes a child may start out feeling a high degree of

affection from one or both parents but after a time begins to experience rejection. The child gradually may realize that the affection he or she is receiving from one or both parents isn't genuine. It could be that, in the beginning, the child actually was a stand-in for the other parent. A mother who doesn't have a good relationship with her husband may transfer her affection to her infant, because the child can't reject either her or the attention she gives. And simply because the object of her attention and affection is an infant, some degree of acceptance and affection naturally is returned. But as the child grows older, the parent no longer considers the child a safe recipient of love, so the attention and affection is withdrawn, sending the message that the child was never loved for himself or herself.

Mothers reject their children for various reasons. Some associate the child, particularly a son, with his father. In the eyes of the mother, the child is the father; and to the extent that the father is hated, the child is hated. The child's own identity is denied because of the mother's strong negative feelings toward the father. If the mother has daughters, they may be favored over sons.

Other mothers find it easier to reject a child than to run the emotional risk of losing the child. Still others feel that a child is the bind that keeps the couple stuck in a bad marriage. The degree of problems in the marriage may influence the amount of rejection toward the child. If the husband is not as attractive as the wife had desired, or if she is abused by him, her rejection of their child could be extreme because she feels locked into the marriage.

If a marriage is shaky and the wife believes that a child will save the marriage, the child may receive conditional acceptance. When the marriage fails to improve because of the presence of the child, he or she may be blamed for the failure. The mother may now feel that she is stuck with a child as well as a husband.[3]

Sometimes favoritism occurs because a parent identifies closely with a child similar to himself or herself. A firstborn father may favor the firstborn son, a middle-born mother may favor her middle-born daughter, and so on. Perhaps a parent mistreated his or her younger siblings, and now these grown siblings favor and protect their youngest. Again, it's like a reenactment of childhood history.

Think back to your family. What about your mother? What was her birth order in her family of origin? What about her parents? What about your father? What was his birth order? And what about his parents? Could there be any correlation between their positions and your own?

Perhaps a mother is convinced that one child is more attractive, easier to raise, more intelligent, creative, cute or looks like her. Sometimes there is no apparent reason. The favoritism of one and the rejection of another just doesn't seem to make sense.

Effects on the Unfavored

At the conclusion of the film *Houdini*, there is a very telling scene. Houdini has just died, and his wife, Bess, and brother are talking. Houdini's brother tells Bess that when his mother died, she was in terrible pain. In agony, she had whispered to Houdini's brother, "I only tried to make him [Houdini] strong. Please ask him to forgive me." Bess then asks, "Why didn't you tell him?" The brother answers, "All my life, he came first in everything. I loved him, Bess, more than he would let me. But at the same time, I hated him. She was my mother, too, and when she died, she didn't have a single word for me."

Mixed feelings toward a favored sibling are not uncommon. It is also not uncommon for an unfavored child to believe that something is wrong with himself or herself rather than with the parents. But favoritism is always the parents' problem, not the child's. I've even worked with some adults who ended up believing their parents were right—the favored sibling *was* better than they were!

> *It is not uncommon for an unfavored child to believe something is wrong with himself or herself rather than with the parents. But favoritism is always the parents' problem.*

As in the case of Houdini's brother, the unfavored child's anger and hatred—even when mixed with love—may not be directed toward the parents. The favored sibling may be the object of retaliation. It's safer to blame a brother or sister than one's parents. Joseph was in this position, but unfortunately both he and his father, Jacob, fueled the situation that elicited anger and jealousy from the older brothers.

What often happens in this sort of situation is a crusade to outdo the favored sibling. This scenario can be created by angry feelings toward the sibling and a desire to gain favor from the parent. You're going to be king of the mountain now and knock that other person off the throne! Remember, though, that by thinking this way, you're still letting your parent control your life. I've seen 40-year-olds still striving to please their parents, and even then it didn't work.

Sometimes a child believes favoritism is occurring when perhaps it isn't. The question is, was it really favoritism or just a sibling perception of it? Most children, out of their feelings of jealousy, will believe their siblings are receiving special treatment. But even if it's just a feeling or perception, if the feeling persists into adulthood, reality is created around those feelings. It will have its negative effect over time. One man who was a favorite of his parents wrote:

> A man who has been the indisputable favorite of his mother keeps for life the feeling of a conqueror, that confidence of success that often indicates real success.[4]

Another famous man, Alfred Adler, who was not his mother's favorite, said:

> Almost every discouragement in childhood springs from the feeling that someone else is preferred. It is not possible for a human being to bear without disgust and irritation the position of being put on a lower level than someone else.[5]

Favoritism is a family plague. It's the source for some of the worst experiences of sibling rivalry. Some parents actually feel that the competition between children teaches them to survive in a competitive world. I've seen families purposely pit one child against another, and there's no one else around to take care of the damage control.

What is needed to avoid these situations are parents who make every effort to avoid preferential treatment of their children, to give consistent and balanced love and acceptance as equally as possible.[6]

All (Should Be) Equal Favorites

One of my closest friends made some comments at his daughter's wedding reception that captured everyone's attention. His daughter is a tall, attractive, fair-skinned blond, and the man she married is tall and black with a shaved head, causing him to resemble some of the more famous basketball players. He had two children from a previous marriage; these two, along with the two children from my friend's other daughter, gave him four grandchildren. At the wedding reception he stood to say a few words. He welcomed his new son-in-law into the family, along with his children. He then said, "We look upon your children as our own grandchildren. Sometimes people ask me if I have a favorite grandchild, and I say, 'No, I don't.' But I thought about it, and that's not true. I do have favorites."

At this point he had everyone's attention, and his wife was looking at him with the "How are you going to get out of this one?" look. He explained, "Our first grandchild is my favorite, since he's the oldest and it's always special to have that first one. But then the next grandson is my favorite because he was named after me. Our two new grandchildren are favorites, too. My new grandson likes to fish like I do, and that makes him a favorite. And our new granddaughter is a favorite since she's the first granddaughter we've ever had." Needless to say, there were tears in the eyes of many of those in attendance.

What would it be like in our families if every child were a favorite in some way, just as he or she is in God's family? God doesn't play favorites. To Him, each one of us is a favorite. We are special—special enough that, in the abundance of love He has for us, He gifted each person with the gift of His Son, Jesus Christ, so that we could have a relationship with a loving, accepting Father.

What about you? Were you an unfavored child? Take a few moments to consider how you would answer these questions:

• What are your feelings toward the favored sibling?
• Do you compete with that sibling in any way?

- Are you still trying and hoping to win your parents' love?
- Why do you believe your sibling ended up being the favorite?
- Whom do you blame for this situation?
- Do you in any way become involved in relationships that repeat your relationship with the favored sibling?
- What steps have you taken to overcome this problem and move on with your life?

Overcoming the Effects of Rejection

If you were the rejected child, there are steps you can take to break the pattern and effects of not being favored. No one likes to be left out, either as a child or as an adult. For some, to be recognized by that neglecting parent can become an obsession. If positive steps don't seem to gain the parent's attention, then attention for misbehaving, or becoming an obnoxious misfit may seem better than no attention at all. Some become sullen, uncooperative and rebellious, which only leads to further rejection. If they can't get any attention on the inside of the family, then there are outside attractions such as gangs, cults, etc.

Some children who are unfavored by one parent will bond or attempt to bond with the other parent if there's any hint of acceptance from that side. Unfortunately, this can turn into emotional enmeshment, which is just as unhealthy as abandonment.

If you were unfavored by a parent, consider these words of hope for your present and your future:

Being unloved by a parent may always leave scars, but the wound can be healed and healthy growth can begin anew. It is worth giving up even those songs and dances that have helped you to survive parental unlovingness because there are better ways to feel okay. In exchanging the old songs and dances for more authentic movement, it is crucial to begin to accept that your parents' not loving you is a statement about them and not about you. In other words, it bespeaks a defect in their ability to love rather than a defect in your lovability. It becomes particularly important to see the child within your parent because it is the inner child, too big a part of your parent, that made him or her unable to love you. If your parent had you to please his own parents, or his spouse, or society, then it was the little child in him trying to do good, the conforming child, trying to get approval or avoid disapproval, that made the decision. You were brought into this world by a child, and children can only play at being loving parents.[7]

Listen to the affirmations and accept the acceptance of others. Look at some pictures of yourself, and list all the positive features you possess. Recognize and accept that the defect is not within you. If there was favoritism in your family, you were raised in an unhealthy and unbiblical family atmosphere.

As you look at your parents and siblings, is your relationship with them a healthy, replenishing one, or is it depleting? If it's continued to be depleting after all your efforts, you may need to distance yourself from some of your family members. Efforts to please those who won't be pleased is an exercise in futility. The rejection you received wasn't and isn't deserved. You may need to look at current relationships and avoid those in which the old patterns are repeated.[8]

If you were rejected by your parents, the problem was not within you but within them. Many parents who reject their children may have been rejected themselves in some way, but they never found a way or took the time to work out their own difficulties. They just directed these onto you. What's important for you to consider is the possibility that you might end up directing your rejection onto others in addition to yourself.

If you experienced rejection from your parents, it could be the rejection occurred because your parents simply were not ready to be parents—they were immature. Most people can conceive and give birth to a child, but that is the easiest part of all. Living with that child, loving that child and meeting that child's needs do not come naturally to everyone. Your parents may have had a deficiency in their capacity or desire to be loving and caring. Parenting takes depth of character, maturity, wisdom and patience. Perhaps these were absent in your parents' makeup.

No matter why you were rejected, it could help you to give your parents permission, in your mind, to have their own expectations of you. You could say to yourself, *It would be nice to have my parents' approval, but it is not earth-shattering if I don't get it. I have God's approval, others' approval and my own approval. I won't be perfect, and I don't have to be perfect, God has taken care of that for me with the gift of His Son.*

One way to move ahead in your life is to acknowledge and then list what your parents expected you to be or do. Likewise, acknowledge what you expected of your parents. Write down your answers to the following questions.

1. What do you believe your parents' expectations of you were or are in order for them to accept you?
2. What are your expectations of yourself? Which of these are really yours and which are coming from parents?
3. What are your expectations for your parents?
4. Which of the expectations listed in number 1 have you discussed with your parents?

5. Have you ever gone to them and shared your feelings of not being accepted? With some parents this is possible and with others it is not. You will have to decide.

Some people continue throughout their lifetime to play the role of a rejected child, but that role carries a high price tag. It is difficult, but vital, to give up your fantasy of having your parents change. If your parents are unhappy, the roots of their unhappiness do not lie in you but in their own past. The deficit isn't in you. You can't make up for what your parents did not receive in their childhoods. You can't undo what has been done to them or to yourself in relationship with them. You can, however, live your own life and allow the presence of Jesus Christ to be the fulfilling source.

Don't open and reopen wounds from your past by behaving now as you used to with your parents or siblings. Look for acceptance, approval and love from those who have the capability of giving those to you. This would include being loving to yourself.

Issues for Favored Children

On the other side of the fence, if you happened to be the favored child, you have your own set of issues. It's true that being favored can strengthen your self-confidence and identity, but it can still exact a price. A preferred sibling may try to lord it over the others, like Joseph did, and we've seen the result of that. Or a favored child could carry a burden of guilt, knowing that a parent's partiality was unfair. The guilt may make a favored child feel obligated in some way, or end up becoming a slave to the approval of the parent.[9]

REMEMBER JOSEPH

You may think it's great to be the favored child. If you do, just remember Joseph. He was bound up, thrown into a pit and sold into slavery. When you're a favorite, you too can become a slave. You may feel locked into your parents' approval, which has its own unique set of limitations. There may be other ways you'd like to respond, but what if that causes disfavor? There's the feeling of always having to produce. You end up feeling that you have to buy your parents' approval by performing. So the answer seems to be to continue to perform or lose out.

OVERWHELMING EXPECTATIONS

There is even more of a downside than meets the eye when you're a favored child. The expectations can sometimes be overwhelming. Fathers have sometimes pushed their sons athletically to become all that they were never able to attain. Some parents fixate on one child who shows academic ability, giving this one every opportunity and advantage while shortchanging the other children. They even may refer to this child as "the smart one" or "the one with the brains." One wealthy family sent their favored child to Harvard and the others to a state school, even though all of them had the academic ability to make it at Harvard.

Often with a favored child the relationship can become enmeshed or too close. When a child is chosen to be the favored one, he or she may develop a compulsive drive to succeed. When a parent or both parents select one child to be the favorite, that child ends up with many privileges. But for every parental privilege, there is probably a hateful or jealous response from another person—usually a sibling.

As a favored child, you could end up expecting the rest of the world to respond to you in the same way your parents did. This leads to constant disappointment.

If you aren't sure why you were the favored one, wondering about it may make you question your strengths and qualities. I've talked to some who have wondered what their parents saw in them, since they can't see it themselves. Parents aren't doing a child any favor by making him or her the favorite.

If you felt as though you were a favored child, consider these questions:

- Do you think you did something special to be a favorite?
- Did you take advantage of this position with your parents in any way?
- How did you treat your unfavored siblings?
- How did you respond when you heard or saw your parents treat your siblings in a rejecting way?
- How has this favored position impacted the way you interact with others? What are your expectations of others?
- Have you discussed your favored position and your siblings' unfavored position with them?
- What steps have you taken to balance out your life and your relationship with your siblings?

Notes
1. Barbara Sullivan, *No Two Alike* (Old Tappan, N.J.: Chosen Books, Fleming H. Revell, 1987), pp. 38, 39.
2. John F. McDermott, Jr., M.D., *Raising Cain (and Abel, Too)* (New York: Wyden Books, distributed by Harper & Row, 1980), p. 82.
3. H. Norman Wright, *Making Peace with Your Past* (Grand Rapids, Mich.: Fleming H. Revell, 1985), p. 86, adapted.
4. Ernest Jones, *The Life and Work of Sigmund Freud,* Vol. I (New York: Basic Books, 1953), n.p.

5. Alfred Adler, edited by Alan Porter, *What Life Should Mean to You* (Boston: Little Brown, 1931), pp. 142, 143.

6. Drs. William and Madra Hapworth and Joan Rathner Heilman, *Mom Loved You Best* (New York: Viking Penguin, 1993), p. 24, adapted.

7. Howard M. Halpern, *Cutting Loose: A Guide to Adult Terms with Your Parents* (New York: Bantam Books, 1977), p. 126.

8. Patti McDermott, *Sisters and Brothers* (Los Angeles: Lowell House, 1992), pp. 81-103, adapted. See also Helene S. Arnstein, *Brothers and Sisters/Sisters and Brothers* (New York: E. P. Dutton, 1979), pp. 9-19, adapted.

9. Ibid., pp. 12, 13, adapted.

Chapter Four

What Role Do You Play?

In Hollywood, California, the movie capital of the world, each primary studio has a department called "major casting." This department primarily is responsible for finding the right people to play certain roles. A call goes out, and many people come in for the auditions. The trick is to meld the various people into a believable and smoothly functioning cast.

Family Labels

A family functions somewhat like a major casting department. Families inevitably cast their members in somewhat predictable roles out of necessity and convenience. It appears that families pass out roles to the children based upon birth order, temperament and gender. But instead of being temporary, some of these casting decisions become permanent. Some roles are healthy and good, while others are not, and many of the roles assigned to children in a family are outgrowths of the labels given to each one.

Labels—they're on everything today. We check labels to verify that the article is the "real thing." When we go to the store for slacks, blouses, shirts or jeans, one of the first things we do is look at the label. We select certain foods in the market based upon the label. Labels are a major part of life.

Unfortunately, we also label people, and those labels, whether accurate or not, seem to follow us into adulthood. One woman told me:

> I not only wear clothes and jewelry with labels, I have a label stamped on me as well. My parents gave it to me, and my siblings made sure it stuck to me, just like their own labels. Sometimes I feel like it's tattooed on my back, and I'm the only one conscious of it until I get around my family. Then it seems like it's plastered all across my forehead for everyone to read. I can't remember a time when I didn't have this label. My parents gave them out to us as early as possible. I guess it made us predictable and helped to give them some security. I have a friend who's an only child. He got labeled, too, but his labels seemed better than the ones I've seen in our family. They were positive. We got some of both— positive and negative.

It's interesting how quickly labels are given to children. Perhaps it's because parents begin to compare them before the siblings themselves are aware of any differences. In the first few months of a child's life, Mom or Dad will say, "He's more alert at this age than she was"; "She's so easygoing compared to him"; "This is the pretty one [fat one, slow one]." It's difficult not to compare, since each subsequent child is seen in contrast to what the parents learned from their first child. This is how they evaluate the development of the next child. Can you imagine what it's like for the fifth child if he or she is compared to the first four?

In time the comparisons evolve into labels, as surely as cocoons turn into butterflies. Some labels are harmless, while others sting. Some are based upon what parents don't see in their child. But labels may overlook who a child really is, as well as that child's true abilities.

A label isn't always a positive means of identification. If it sticks, a label is like an ointment rubbed onto the skin. In time it penetrates deeper. Labels become part of children's perceptions of themselves. They begin to see themselves in light of their labels, and this is incorporated into the roles they play in life.

Parents aren't being malicious in giving labels. Often the labels are given to emphasize the positive attributes or strengths of a child or to limit rivalry or jealousy between siblings. There's nothing wrong with introducing a child as "the helper" or "the caring child" or "the arbitrator" or "the musician of the family." But labels can become self-fulfilling prophecies. Perhaps as an adult, living up to that label isn't healthy, or the adult simply doesn't want to have to live up to it anymore.[1]

Changed His Label, Changed His Destiny

You're probably familiar with the name Mark Twain. Most of us have read his books about Tom Sawyer and Huck Finn. But Mark Twain was not his real name. It was Samuel Clemens. Samuel had been labeled as a boy who always got into mischief. He was told in front of his brothers and sisters that he was a problem child, a troublemaker. But he didn't want to have that label follow him throughout his life, so he ran away from home, hoping to become someone whom others would be proud of one day.

Samuel joined the men who worked the riverboats. There he created his characters Tom Sawyer and Huck Finn. He turned his adventures into stories, finding great satisfaction in his life on the river. Eventually he even changed his name. On the river there was a call: "Quarterless Twain! By the Mark! M-a-a-rk Twain." He felt the name fit him somehow, so he took it as his own.

As Samuel Clemens, he fulfilled the role created for him in the family. We'd probably call him a rebel or scapegoat today. But using the river as his new family, and changing his name to Mark Twain, he became a hero by providing us with some of the greatest American literature ever written.[2]

> *If we behave like our labels, we can turn them into reality. We can even learn to use them as convenient excuses for our shortcomings and character flaws.*

Ideally speaking, there should be no labels in families, but we don't live in an ideal world. And labels do tend to become who we really are in some ways, even if we don't like it. If we behave like our labels, we can turn them into reality. We can even learn to use them to our advantage so that they become convenient excuses for our shortcomings and character flaws. If a sibling challenges us for our label, we may invest time and energy to hang on to what we consider to be ours.

Identifying Labels

Some families place higher value on certain labels. This can lead to favoritism. Did you have a label as a child? Do you still have it today? If so, what do you think it might be like not to have a label? Has your label been a liability or an asset? Do you remember how others used to refer to you? Has that changed? What words would you use to describe yourself today? What words would your siblings select? What were your siblings' labels? Who in your family was bothered most by labels? Here's a list of words to help you reflect on terms that may have been used for you or your siblings. See what you can remember about them:

Intelligent Unintelligent Athletic Unathletic
Creative Artistic Attractive Beautiful Plain
Obedient Rebellious Nonconforming Ordinary
Quiet Idealistic Materialistic Pragmatic
Opportunistic Pessimistic Optimistic Angry
Cheerful Charismatic Depressed Self-Righteous
Greedy Irritable Shy Aggressive Manipulative
Outgoing Even-tempered Self-Contained
Self-Sufficient Charming Competitive Industrious
Cooperative Organized Disorganized Critical
Responsible Irresponsible Understanding Driven
Punitive Accepting Lazy Good Bad
Honorable Underhanded Gregarious Moral
Asocial Devious Straightforward Practical Cool
Talkative Enthusiastic Assertive Feisty Calm
Generous Curious Interfering Envious
Self-critical Competent Incompetent Leader
Follower Loner Well-Mannered Rude
Gentle Abrasive Introverted Thrifty[3]

Even though you may not like the role you had as a child, it was deeply engraved on your memory. You are familiar with your own script and how the other family members played different parts. These roles will tend to follow you the rest of your life unless you engage in some major surgery. You'll replay these same scripts over and over again. And whether you realize it or not, you tend to be attracted to others who play, and let you play, the roles you know best. As you think of your family as the cast for a movie, who had the lead? Who had the supporting roles? Who was the hero and who was the villain?

Roles by themselves aren't good or bad. It's the way you express them that determines whether they are healthy or not. Healthy roles help you accept and feel good about yourself, whereas unhealthy roles feed your despair and low self-esteem. A 47-year-old man told me:

> I've always wondered how my three brothers and I got our role assignments. I wondered if there was a list of these roles, and when each of us was born, our parents took out the list and debated it for a few days before assigning our parts. In fact, we each know we have a distinct role; we accept the fact and even joke about it. Sometimes, before family get-togethers, we call one another and switch roles just to mess up our parents and other relatives. It's a lot of fun for us, but it sure confuses them. They're not sure how to respond, and even though we've planned it all out, we find ourselves slipping back to who we really are in a couple of hours. I guess this is who we'll always be to some degree. It's as though they're permanent assignments from a teacher.

Variations Within Roles

Roles aren't all the same in their expressions. There are variations on themes, just as there are variations in certain piano pieces. The melody is always there, but it's presented differently. A caretaker role could be expressed in a gentle, caring, kind manner, or it could be expressed by a tyrant who wants to dominate everyone.

Your role helps you know how to respond during stress, just as your sense of identity helps you function in everyday life. Your role gives clarity to why you respond the way you do, and it gives others a sense of security in responding to you. They see you and think, "Oh, here's John, the rebel [caretaker, hero, pleaser]," and know what to expect and how to respond to you.[4]

Roles Can Provide Balance

Roles also give your family an identity and some sense of balance. But when one person makes a radical change or suddenly leaves, that intricate balance is immediately upset. A change could be something like failing a course, using drugs or becoming a Christian and changing your values. Unless some sort of regrouping and recasting is accomplished at that point, a family could be in danger of going out of business.

Some roles have prescribed duties, such as mother, father, grandparent, brother or sister. Each different culture usually has its own script for most of the formal roles of a family. But are you aware that every family plays out a series of informal roles as well? These more spontaneous and casual scripts develop in order to maintain the balance within a family and to reduce tension. Some of those informal roles occur because of unique personality differences and birth-order characteristics.[5]

Let's consider a few of these informal roles to help you better understand your past and present family members. Remember too that each role seems to carry with it a feeling or emotion.

THE MEDIATOR

A family usually has a mediator, an individual everyone turns to when a problem needs to be settled. Others see him or her as the person who is fair. In most families, this person is a parent, but in some it could be a child. This individual is a problem solver. One man told me, "I feel like a court arbitrator. I'm constantly helping my family resolve their issues. Oh well, at least it brings a sense of calm to our family." He was very sensitive and had difficulty dealing with his two oldest siblings and the intensity of their fights.

Did your family of origin enlist the help of a mediator? Who was it? Is that person still playing this role today in family get-togethers? How well did he or she do the job? If no one qualified as mediator, did chaos reign? Who is the mediator in your present family? How comfortable are you with this current arrangement? What if something happened to your current family mediator? Would the other family members be able to resolve serious problems on their own? If a family doesn't have a mediator, others (such as the family clown, scapegoat, crybaby, or enabler), may jump in to reduce tension.[6]

THE ENTERTAINER

Some siblings serve in the role of entertainer. It's as if they barge into the room with a dramatic flare, singing, "Let me entertain you." Entertainers are on center stage, with or without an audience. At times they pour forth a steady stream of chatter, regardless of whether or not anyone is listening or responding. Entertainers orchestrate the family's social life, including where, when and how. They are the family's link to the outside world because of their contacts with others.

Who fit this role in your family? If it was a sibling, has this role been carried over to his or her own family? What about your present family? Is there an entertainer in your midst? How do the other family members feel about this person?

THE ENABLER

Enablers provide emotional and relational nurture and a sense of belonging. Since they usually want to preserve the family unity at all costs, they often go to extremes to keep the peace. Their goal is to eliminate all conflicts and help everyone get along. Unfortunately, with an enabler in control, conflicts are more often buried and perpetuated rather than resolved. Enablers tend to be driven by fear. They are afraid that family members cannot survive without their efforts, as well as fearing that others will abandon them.

Jim was a middle child who described his role so well: "I feel like I belong to a United Nations peacekeeping team whose job is to put out all the small wars that erupt throughout the world, and then maintain the peace."

Was there an enabler in your family of origin? If so, who was it? Was it a sibling? If you were the enabler, do you carry any resentment because of the price tag attached to such a role? Can you think of any conflicts that got ceremoniously swept under the rug? Who has assumed that role in your present family? Can you see the underlying fear that motivates such behavior? Would you like to make any changes in how this role functions in your own life?

THE DOER

The doer in your family was the one who said, "Give it to me and it will get done." Doers have an overdeveloped sense of responsibility that often drives them unmercifully. They provide most of the maintenance functions in a family. Doers also are referred to as the responsible ones who make sure bills are paid, people are fed, clothed, chauffeured and so on. Sometimes they take this sense of responsibility too far and try to orchestrate the lives of other family members.

We usually remember the doers in our family of origin because they always took up the slack. Who assumed this role in your growing-up years? How did your family benefit from his or her efforts? Did that person carry that sense of responsibility gracefully, or did he or she tend to whine about the unfair distribution of labor in the family? Are there any doers in your present family? Do you like this present arrangement? If not, what changes would you like to make?

HEROES AND CARETAKERS

Heroes can be doers or caretakers. A hero's success and achievement bring recognition and prestige to the family. A hero becomes addicted to pleasing others. Sometimes the hero fulfills the family dream, adopting it as his or her own. The esteem the hero receives builds up the rest of the family.

Remember, a caretaker or hero is an overly responsible child whose dominant emotion usually is depression—a baseball infielder who is asked to play all four infield positions at the same time. There are too many demands and not enough resources to go around, so the hero or caretaker ends up feeling overwhelmed and depressed. This sense of overresponsibility is the child's attempt to dispel the family shame.

One of the most damaging roles is when the overly responsible child becomes the parentified (taking on the characteristics and responsibilities of a parent) child. When this happens, it is often due to a lack of intimacy between the parents. They're together yet they function more like a pair of singles than a closely connected couple. Some children in these situations end up thwarting their own childhood development by taking on a hyper-responsible role as a surrogate spouse to one of their parents or as a parent to themselves and/or their siblings. This is asking too much of a child. It's no wonder that some heroes either become super-responsible or want nothing to do with responsibility when they grow up. Did anyone in your family assume this role?

THE CLOWN

The family clown brings humor into the family through play, fun and even silliness. The clowns are always joking and cutting up, especially when confronted by difficult situations. Their fun-loving nature is a great cover-up for any deep pain or isolation. Humor brings the attention clowns may feel unable to merit in other areas. One man told me, "I always got a lot of attention. Even when Mom was really upset with me, I'd get off the hook. I could always make her laugh."

Clowns usually are the most lovable ones, but often at great cost to themselves. Are there any clowns in your past family? Do they still make you laugh and feel good? What about your present family? What do you see as some of the results of having a clown in the family? What is your family clown's place in the birth order of your family?

THE MANIPULATOR

Manipulators are the clever controllers in the family who learned early on how to get others to do what they wanted. They know how to seduce, charm, play sick or appear weak. They can and often do use every trick in the book to get their way.

Think back. Does any sibling come to mind who played that role during your childhood years? What feelings arose if you were among those being manipulated? Do you have any unresolved anger or resentment? Do you experience manipulation in your present family? Is this role clearly focused on anyone in particular? How do you feel about this person?

THE CRITIC

Critics are the faultfinding negativists who always see the glass as half empty instead of half full. Their behavior is characterized by sarcasm, hurtful teasing and complaining. They prefer to use their energy to tear others down rather than build them up. Critics are not very pleasant to be around, but some families end up enduring them.

Think about your past family. What about Mom? Dad? Siblings? Grandparents? Children? Any painful memories of unfair criticism? Some families are so permeated with faultfinding that not even the tiniest mistake escapes notice. Did you ever feel like you were walking around on eggshells? Is there a critic in your present family? In what ways is this person fulfilling a destructive or perhaps a useful role? What can be done to improve this situation?

THE SCAPEGOAT

Scapegoats are the family victims who actually end up as the family blame collectors. The victim's misbehavior makes everyone else's behavior look good, causing the rest of them to think that if it weren't for the scapegoat, the family would be just about perfect.

Each role fulfills a specialized function within the family, and the scapegoat is no exception. If family members are angry with one another and have their weapons out, ready to fire, the scapegoat stands up and says, "Here I am. You can all shoot at me"—which they usually do! This child willingly draws the fire in order to protect everyone else. It's as though the scapegoat walks around wearing a sign that says "Anger container—dump here."

This child can either draw in the anger or act it out. If the scapegoat tries to change roles, the family may not let him or her off the hook. As long as the scapegoat is around, the rest of the family members have someone to blame for their own irresponsibility.

The term "scapegoat" is a biblical one. In the Old Testament, two goats were used in the sacrificial worship that atoned for the people's sins. One of the goats was chosen by lot to be the scapegoat. It was symbolically laden with all the sins and wrongdoings of the people. Then it was sent away into the wilderness. The other goat, which was seen as pure, was set aside as a special offering to the Lord.

Families carry out a similar procedure. They have one particularly good child, and the other children's deeds are contrasted to this one. In this process, one child often begins to be seen as the scapegoat. All the bad stuff is dumped on him or her, and that child is then viewed and treated as an outsider. This child is singled out by the parents as the worst child, and the other siblings may follow in their rejection of the scapegoat.

Sometimes it is just one parent who sees the child in this way. But that's all it takes. In many cases, not only is the scapegoat child unable to change the situation, but neither are the siblings or the other parent.

We hear a great deal about incompatibility. We have incompatibility between married couples, and there can even be a mismatch between a person and a pet. You also can find incompatibility between a parent and child. Perhaps you saw the movie *A River Runs Through It.* This story came from a novel by Norman Maclean; it was a memoir about Paul, Norman's youngest brother. Paul and his father had a mismatch of temperaments and personalities. The father was a strict Presbyterian minister. He and Paul engaged in tremendous power struggles. Norman Maclean describes a particular situation this way:

My mother and I watched horrified morning after morning while the Scottish minister tried to make his small child eat oatmeal. My father was also horrified—at first because a child of his own bowels would not eat God's oats, and, as the days went on, because his wee child proved tougher than he was. As the minister raged, the child bowed his head over the food and folded his hands as if his father were saying grace. . . . The hotter my father got, the colder the porridge. . . . [7]

When parents expect to be in charge and want compliance from their children, a certain child's stubbornness may be so upsetting that, in the parents' eyes, the child is seen and treated as a problem.[8]

I've seen families in which parents refer to their child as being "just like his Uncle Bill. You know, my youngest brother who was such a pain when I was growing up." It seemed the parents were reenacting their own sibling issues and creating their son in the image of a brother.

A disliked child doesn't have many coping resources to resist the pressure. Thus, it's easier to become, in fact, what parents see in the child. (Many children truly are rebellious by their own nature; they don't need any help or nudge in that direction by anyone else.)

Ralph grew up as a scapegoat, although he didn't use that term. Instead, he referred to himself as "the black sheep" of his family. He had an interesting statement about his role:

I don't know why I got dumped on so much. I don't think I did that much that warranted all that reaction. Even my brothers and sisters couldn't see it. But it kept getting worse. After a while I guess it was easier to be the

way they saw me, because what I tried to do to change
my image never worked. Not being the way they saw me
was worse than not being successful at being good. It
doesn't make sense, but it felt better.[9]

Even though scapegoats don't seem to care about what's going
on, they actually tend to be the most sensitive people in the family.
Because they are sensitive, they notice the hurt in the family and
often act out the resulting stress through misbehavior. Their negative actions may be a cry to the rest of the family to do something
about the hurtful things that are happening in the home.

When scapegoats are the children in the family, they often
feel responsible for keeping their parents' marriage together. If
they sense problems between the adults, they may use misbehavior in an effort to draw the parents together to deal with the
errant behavior.

Scapegoating is very destructive. Unfortunately, these victims learn when to take the blame, sometimes purposefully creating situations in which they can be blamed in order to reduce
tension in the family. Scapegoating can be predicted to some
degree. If it happened in your family of origin, it will tend to be
carried on in your present family. Families tend to scapegoat
someone when they are insecure about themselves or their
authority. It's a way to suppress their own feelings of inferiority.

June was the middle of five children. Her mother got along
fairly well with the other four, but from the time June was a tod-
dler, the two of them were at odds. June was not the beautiful,
perfect child that her mother had wanted or expected. She was
fussy and picky with her food. Her mother came to see June as
demanding, stubborn and controlling. So when anything went
wrong, who got blamed? June, of course. After a while, the other
children began to notice this pattern and joined in. They discov-

ered they could get away with all kinds of violations by implicating June as the culprit. In time, June became the scapegoat. It became a life of deception for her siblings and a life of misery for her. She believed she was bad. And when you believe something about yourself, you often tend to behave accordingly. It's one way to get attention, even if it takes a toll.

Scapegoating also may be determined by the birth order of the parents. Firstborn parents are likely to protect their own firstborn; second-born parents will protect their second-born, and so on. A child from a difficult labor or a handicapped child may be protected, while the other children are cast into the scapegoat role.[10]

Did someone serve as a scapegoat in your family of origin? Can you see how they collected the family garbage, even unintentionally? What useful purpose did they fulfill? How do you think they may have suffered as a result? Who is the usual scapegoat in your present family? Has that person ever expressed a desire to step out of that role? Do any changes need to happen in this area of your family life?[11]

Assigning Roles

How do roles get assigned to family members? Many factors may come into play, such as family expectations, birth order, gender or the changing needs of the family. Even physical resemblances or personality characteristics that remind people of another relative may play a significant part in assigning roles.

One of the best descriptions of family role assignment is found in *Mom Loved You Best*. Consider what the authors say and where you fit into this description:

> You are cast in your role in the family through an intricate psychological process, directed by forces that are

almost always unconscious and often fraught with powerfully conflicted emotions. The roles are delegated according to the parents' needs, the children's actual abilities and labels, and the mother's and father's views of these traits. At the same time, they are intended to promote the family values that, projected onto the children, form an agenda for the next generation.

> *How do roles get assigned to family members? Sometimes they emerge to help the parents avoid re-creating their own childhood. In other cases, the parents may actually want to re-create it.*

The children are expected to accept their roles, internalize them, and accommodate them, after trying them on for size and fit and looking for parts they can play. In most cases, they take to the roles that feel right to them, the ones that suit their natural abilities and give them some status and clout within the group.

Siblings as well as parents have an important influence on what roles each of them takes, unwittingly encouraging, demanding, cajoling one another into them. Just by looking up to a big sister who takes care of them and admiring her abilities to cope with crises, for example, younger siblings can make her feel it is suitable for her to take on responsibility while the others have fun.[12]

Sometimes roles emerge to help the parents avoid re-creating their own childhood. In other cases, the parents actually may want to re-create it. Sometimes there's a hierarchy of importance to a role. A hero may be the most important for some families, whereas for others it could be a pleaser. Some prefer a scapegoat, since they then have a dumping ground for their problems.

COMPARISONS

Have you ever been compared to, or compared someone else to, a family member?

- You're just like your father.
- You look and talk just like Uncle Lyle.
- You remind me so much of my sister when she was your age.

Naming a child after someone also tends to generate comparisons. Even the selection of a particular name may cast a person in a particular role.[13]

GENDER

Is gender a factor in who ends up with certain roles, or is this an equal opportunity process? Actually, boys are more likely to end up as scapegoats, while girls are more likely to be heroes or caretakers or even take on parentified roles. A mediator or a lost child, which we will discuss in a moment, can be either sex.

BIRTH ORDER

We've talked about the significance of birth order elsewhere, but roles are no respecter of the birth-order structure. Still, where you rank in the birth order has some bearing on what role you may have had. Who would you expect to end up being the hero or caretaker? If you guessed the oldest, you're right—most of the time, that is. However, if you were the oldest and a male in a family where males were not really favored, you were probably passed over for this role, and its mantle was placed on the oldest female sibling. Then you ended up being the lost child, the one who didn't know where you fit. This would be an exception, because the lost child is more likely to be the middle or younger child than the oldest.

Why would a middle child end up as the lost child? I like the illustration I heard from one man:

> I'm a middle child. I feel like the back wheels on my car. No matter how fast I go, I never catch up with the front wheels. I'll never catch up with my older brother either. Not only that, my younger brother had a much easier time. Our folks cut him more slack than I got. I feel like an orange in a juicer—squeezed from the top and squeezed from the bottom.

If a middle child tries to hold the oldest and the youngest together in a conflictual family, he or she never feels connected and constantly lives with the fear of being abandoned. And if the older and younger sibling are quite older and younger and/or a different gender, there may be little closeness among any of the siblings.

If a middle child is in a large family (five siblings or more), it's even more difficult to find an identity. What if you have two older and two younger, or even three or four of each? Perhaps all the good characteristics or roles, such as smartest, most attractive, most talented, athletic, funny or mechanical have already been taken. What's left?

In larger families, there are more comparisons and more competition, and it's easier to get lost. Some are raised in what we call a gender-skewed family. If you are the only-gender child in a family with three, four, five or more siblings of the opposite gender, this can affect how you feel about your own gender, either positively or negatively.

An only child can end up playing all the roles. There's no sibling who can excel in clowning, scapegoating or enabling. You could be the hero with all A's and still be the scapegoat when you wreck the car. One man said, "I was the only child, and the best way to describe my situation was the Levi's ad on TV. It showed a pair of Levi's with two sets of mules pulling on the Levi's from either side. That's what I felt like—tugged one way by one parent and another by the other."[14]

What About Your Family?

Let's consider your family relationships. On the following chart, list the names and ages of your siblings, along with the pertinent information about each person. Then indicate as best you can which roles you think each person fits.

My Family

Roles

Mother's birth order _____ _____

Father's birth order _____ _____

Birth order of siblings _____ _____

_____ _____

_____ _____

_____ _____

After looking at your family in this way, can you see how this information may clarify how and why you relate the way you do to others in your adult life?

What might happen to your family balance and dynamics if one sibling gave up his or her role and then either chose another role or didn't play a role at all?

Often the various roles hold a family structure together. Some families are so inflexible that they don't allow for any change in the assigned roles. The children are then more likely to perpetuate those same roles in their future families. I've seen the youngest child in a family referred to as "my little baby" by the parents—even after "the baby" was well past 30! Do you have any memories like this involving yourself or your siblings?

Fortunately, some families become aware of their tendency to cast people in various roles and, as a result, decide to allow family members greater flexibility. This is a healthy move! Sometimes pet names or nicknames are purposely dropped at a certain age. A child may ask to be called by a different name or even declare that he or she is tired of being the one to solve all the problems. Parents often make a declaration of what they will continue to do and what they will no longer be doing within the family.

Childhood roles have a multitude of effects upon each one of us. Some adults who were asked to share their reaction to the role they were assigned in their families said:

- I was ashamed of what I did or had to do. I still am.
- I just laughed it off. I made it work for me.
- Actually, I was proud of it. It worked for me.
- It stunted me. I still feel stuck in my life.
- I didn't know I had a role. I just thought all this stuff was normal.

Sometimes you like your role, sometimes you don't, as the above comments so obviously illustrate.

Some roles we perpetuate, learning how to work them and use them to our advantage. Some roles seem obsolete. They're not needed anymore, because we're not the same people anymore.

Some roles are positive and serve us well as adults, while some stifle us, limiting our potential. Remember, if you were given a label and a role as a child and it has followed you into adulthood, it doesn't mean you are what the label describes; these roles and labels are not cast in stone.

So You Want to Change Your Role

If you want to change your family role, don't expect positive feedback from your sibling—or anyone else for that matter—who knows and responds to you based upon your role. Change is painful, especially when it's initiated by you and forced upon the others. Your siblings probably benefited by your being who you were, and they don't want that benefit taken away, even if the role gives you problems.

If you give up your role, who's going to fill the vacancy, especially when you're an adult? If your role is one of five foundations that keeps your family of origin supported, what happens when that support is taken away? The structure begins to tilt. Stability is gone. Your role could be critical for your family's survival, right or wrong, good or bad. You may want to change, but they fight the change. You may want to grow and mature into a healthier role, yet still they resist you. Somewhere you have a decision to make.

Tom was both a scapegoat and the acting-out rebel in his family. It started when he was in preschool. He took the blame for a lot that wasn't his fault, and for a lot that was. As a teenager he drank, used drugs and dropped out of school. After a divorce in his early twenties, he became a committed Christian and his life was totally turned around. He finished high school and college. His reactions to his siblings were also new—positive but totally upsetting. Since none of them were Christians, they didn't understand this change or believe it would last. They did their best to push him back to his old roles, but nothing worked. Everyone was uncomfortable, and they began to exclude Tom from their lives because of their discomfort. Eventually, they also became Christians and finally understood what had happened to him and why.

You don't have to be held hostage to the past. Although you can't change your past, you do have something to say about the family you have or will have. Looking at your family of origen history will help you determine what you want and don't want for the future. Are you comfortable with the roles you play in relationship to your spouse, your children or other significant people in your life? What ways of responding would you like to give up or change? You may want to write out the role you would like to play and then start to rehearse a different script.

One sibling shared with me his decision to change:

> I began to envision not being a critic anymore. I actually wrote out in advance how I really wanted to respond, wrote out positive, encouraging comments, practiced saying them out loud, prayed about the change, and in time it worked! The hardest part was being consistent and not letting others force me back into the old role.

Gleaning the Best

We are heavily influenced by our upbringing, and we tend to repeat patterns of parenting, whether we want to or not. But we can choose to glean the best from our past experiences and toss out the rest. Why not use the best and the worst lessons from your family of origin as fodder for the future? Evaluate and then select and envision how you would like to respond to your siblings now, as well as how you would like to respond to your own family.

Remember that when you were a child, you saw your parents and siblings through childish eyes. Now you have the opportunity to reevaluate what occurred in your childhood through an adult's eyes.

Notes

1. Francine Klagsbrun, *Mixed Blessings* (New York: Bantam Books, 1992), p. 34, adapted.
2. Joseph Mersand, ed., *Great American Short Biographies* (New York: Dell Publishing Co., 1966), adapted, n.p.
3. Drs. William and Madra Hapworth and Joan Rathner Heilman, *Mom Loved You Best* (New York: Viking Penguin, 1993), pp. 70-80, adapted.
4. Hapworth and Heilman, *Mom*, pp. 83-90, adapted.
5. For additional information on personality differences and birth order characteristics, see *The Power of a Parent's Words* by H. Norman Wright (Ventura, Calif.: Regal Books, 1991).
6. Mel Roman and Patricia E. Raley, *The Indelible Family* (New York: Rawson, Wade Publishers, 1980), pp. 35-39, adapted.
7. Norman Maclean, *A River Runs Through It and Other Stories* (Chicago: University of Chicago Press, 1976), p. 7.
8. Francine Klagsbrun, *Mixed Feelings* (New York: Bantam Books, 1992), pp. 178-81, adapted.
9. Ibid., pp. 184, 85, adapted.
10. Roman and Raley, *Indelible*, pp. 46, 47, adapted.
11. H. Norman Wright, *Always Daddy's Girl* (Ventura, Calif.: Regal Books, 1989), pp. 168, 69, adapted.
12. Hapworth and Heilman, *Mom*, p. 89.
13. Roman and Raley, *Indelible*, pp. 42, 43, adapted.
14. Lorie Dwinell and Ruth Baetz, *We Did the Best We Could* (Deerfield, Fla.: Health Communications, 1993), pp. 90-94, adapted.

Chapter Five

Rivals for Life

Sibling rivalry? It started for me when I was four, and my brother wasn't even born yet. He was still in the womb. My parents kept talking about this "new arrival" that was on the way. They wanted it; I didn't. I was content. I had them all to myself, and then he arrived, all mouth and noise. He latched on to me, and I didn't have a moment's peace. We fought. I'd blame him, and he'd blame me. We were always competing for something, mainly attention. That was 40 years ago. We're grown up now. We're adults, and we still do it.

Competition between siblings—sibling rivalry—exists to some extent in almost every family unit. Sibling rivalry is almost synonymous with the thought of siblings. Competition can be subtle or blatant, slight skirmishes or major wars. You read about this rivalry in all types of literature—in tabloids, books, the newspaper, the Bible. Some say that rivalry is abnormal and unhealthy. Others say it's a part of life, whether in families, in societies or between nations.

Competitive feelings can be observed between those as young as an eighteen-month-old and his or her three-year-old brother. Most of these feelings are resolved through the years. But one of the major hindrances to healthy adult relationships between siblings is unresolved childhood competitive feelings. After reaching adulthood, these siblings have not stopped comparing themselves to one another.

Is there any child who doesn't think he or she is getting the worst end of the deal? I like this parent's insights on the issue:

> Sibling rivalry is natural, but I find it hard to discipline. We all talk about it, and my husband and I try to stress to each child that God gave them all talents, He made them all different, and each is loved as much as the others. But, please don't ask the oldest. He's sure he's been overprotected and has had to sacrifice more and more as each of his four siblings arrived. Then again, don't ask our second son. He knows for sure that our oldest is definitely spoiled and that we are prouder of him than we are of our second born. Our daughter will tell you that, even though she's the middle child and the only girl, in no way is she spoiled. According to her, the boys get everything. Sibling #4 will say he is overlooked, while all the rest say that he is the most spoiled. Last, but not least, our youngest says he's "scrubbed the most." By this, he means that when all the others are taken care of, then we worry about taking care of him. When the chips are down or an emergency occurs, though, they do seem to forget all this and pull together to help each other.[1]

Competitive feelings are there, although they can be hidden or overt. This usually depends on how the parents responded to competition between their children. If the children learned to be sneaky about their competitiveness, there can be denial on the part of one or both siblings.

Wrangling Siblings Achieved the Wright Stuff

Whenever you fly on an airplane, you do so as the result of the rivalry between two brothers. When Wilbur and Orville Wright were 11 and 7, their father brought home a present for them. Did you get that? He brought them a present—one. You'd think he would have known better. The toy was a sort of helicopter—actually, a bat—that flew with the aid of rubber bands. The brothers were fascinated with it, and as brothers do, they fought over the gift. Their father encouraged them to study it and build better ones. They accepted this challenge and worked on it for years. They argued over everything—the design, how a bird soars, how the wings are shaped when outstretched and everything else you can imagine. One brother would come up with an idea, and then the other brother would come up with a better one. On it went until 1903, when Orville climbed into the plane he and Wilbur had built and actually flew for 12 seconds. Their rivalry had been channeled into a constructive venture.[2]

Some families encourage sibling rivalry. Parents feel it's good for the children to compete, that it toughens them. They actually believe they're helping their children improve, even though they may create adverse effects upon the siblings' relationships. Who wants to hear praise of another while you're receiving nothing? Who wants to be told, "You're not as smart [attractive, successful] as your brother"? Labeling often enters in at this point. A child may be referred to as "the bookworm," "the jock," "the slow-poke." Some children learn to win, no matter what. Losing must be avoided at all costs! Some thrive on competition, while others shun it. Unfortunately, none of these children learn how to win or lose gracefully. They can't just do their best and be satisfied. They need to defeat someone, even as an adult.

Oscar's Revenge

In her autobiography, *No Bed of Roses,* actress Joan Fontaine described her bitter relationship with her actress sister, Olivia de Haviland. From birth on, their parents and nurses encouraged them to be rivals. Since they both became actresses, their career choice heightened their competition. This rivalry pushed them to achieve, but it also eroded their relationship even further. In 1941, Joan, along with five others, was nominated for an Oscar. When she heard her named called as the winner, she froze in her chair. Her older sister, Olivia, was at the next table. In a commanding voice, Olivia whispered, "Get up there. Get up there!" Joan's reaction was more of a flashback. She thought of all the animosity she and Olivia had felt toward one another as children, the wrestling matches and hair pulling, the time her sister broke her collarbone, and she felt paralyzed. She had won an Oscar, while her sister had missed out on one the year before. She felt as if Olivia would reach over and attack her. She didn't, of course, and five years later, Olivia finally won her own Oscar. When Joan went over to congratulate her, Olivia took one look at her, ignored her outstretched hand, clutched her Oscar and turned her back on her.[3]

An extreme case, of course, but what about you and your sibling relationships? Does Joan and Olivia's story strike any familiar chords? Perhaps these questions will help clarify the competitiveness in your own family:

- As a child, did you experience competition for a parent's love or attention? If so, from whom?

- As an adult, does that competition still exist? If so, with whom?
- Is there a sibling in your family who still tries to outdo another?
- Did any sibling in your family give up on something because another sibling seemed better at it?
- Who might you feel competitive with now (siblings, spouse, coworkers)?
- Who in your family avoids competition?
- Do you feel comfortable with competition, or do you tend to avoid it?[4]

Parent-Generated Rivalries

One of the worst types of sibling rivalry is that generated by competitive parents who continue their own competition through their children. Some parents feel they have to win to feed their egos. Sadly, their children usually end up feeling the same way. When children are considered reflections of their parents, they live with tremendous pressure, which overshadows cooperation with siblings. Each feels the need to outdo the others. This atmosphere produces children who are desperate for compliments and recognition. This pattern is carried into adult relationships such as marriage and work. I've seen siblings whose sense of competition is so strong that they bet on who can run to the store the fastest, drink the most, catch the most fish, eat the most, be the most obnoxious, etc. There don't appear to be any limits.

Macho Motivations

Although it is true that sisters as well as brothers compete, competition among men is almost part of their gender role. It is their way to prove their competence and establish their status in relationship to others. Even as adults, most male siblings compete. One study showed that almost half of all male siblings between the ages of 22 and 93 still competed with their brothers, not only over such issues as parental favoritism but also over achievements, intelligence, fitness and physical attractiveness. It's interesting to note that brothers see themselves as initiating more rivalry than sisters. (Sisters see brothers doing this as well.)

Brothers are more apt than sisters to admit to competition. It seems to be more frightening for sisters to make this admission. Men are motivated by the desire to be first, with the concern that others may get too close. Women tend to be guided by the desire to be at the center of relationships, with the fear of being left out.[5]

What about the degree of competition between yourself and your siblings? To help you decide, use the line graph below. Indicate the level of competition on the line by placing an X to reflect your childhood and a Y to reflect your current relationship.

1		5		10
NO COMPETITION	VERY LITTLE	AVERAGE	MORE THAN AVERAGE	INTENSE COMPETITION

After seeing this graph, some have expressed surprise over discovering the fact that they grew up in a competitive atmosphere. When you put something in black and white, it takes on a different perspective.

Rivalry is expressed in many ways. Hitting, pinching, giving intimidating or sarcastic looks, embarrassing the rival, cajoling, teasing, tattling, bragging and lying are all effective tools for downgrading another and elevating yourself.

Why Kids Compete

Children basically want two things when they compete with one another. First, they want to hang on to their emotional and physical source of nourishment—their parents. When a parent tells a child to "be fair and share," it often falls on deaf ears. Most adults know the meaning of this phrase, for they know that if they share a bit and give a little, they have the assurance that what they have left will remain theirs. Children think differently. They're afraid that if they give up a small amount, they could lose it all. In a sense, a sibling can then be seen as an enemy.

> *Children basically want two things when they compete with one another: to hang on to their emotional and physical source of nourishment— their parents—and to have power and prestige in relation to other siblings.*

Another reason for competition and rivalry between siblings is the desire for power and prestige in relation to other siblings. The feeling is ingrained throughout our society: "Be on top"; "Be number one"; "Don't let others dominate you."[6]

PARENTS

Some parents foster competition. If a parent(s) places excessive demands upon a child (or all the children), the child's desire is to be number one in that parent's eyes. It doesn't matter what siblings think; it's what the parent thinks that counts. This atmosphere creates children who are afraid to trust or confide in their siblings. Their motto becomes "Don't let them into your life. They'll use whatever they know about you against you and to further their own cause." In these families, children learn to live constantly on guard and to be overly protective. "Trust no one if you want to get ahead" is their belief as they grow and move into adult relationships. When you compete with a sibling, you spend more time noticing the achievements of the other person than your own.

Remember that competition exists only if both people play the game! Distancing yourself from the relationship and disengaging from attempts to get baited into competing, or lured into a competitive dialogue, can change the game playing between yourself and your sibling.

There are other parents who don't foster competition, but are stingy with any compliments or praise they give. So the children learn to compete for whatever "table scraps" may be available. They do anything for a word of encouragement, for recognition, for love, and they don't mind trampling on their brother or sister to get what they want.

John McDermott, in his book on sibling rivalry titled *Raising Cain (and Abel Too),* gives this advice:

> Fighting between brothers and sisters is fierce in the first four or five years of life. Then, you must settle conflicts for them. . . . But if you ignore the rivalry that comes with having two or more children, your kids stay locked in battle with each other and even extend their hostilities to the outside world, to their relationships with others, as a way of life.[7]

OTHER LEADERS

Sometimes it's not parents who foster competition. It also can come from teachers or those in church. As a result, younger siblings of firstborn children who seem to have it all—athletic ability, looks, friends, personality—end up living in their shadow. It's not the sibling who creates the problem; it's other people who keep giving recognition to the firstborn, particularly if the other siblings don't have the same attributes as the oldest. They hear comments like, "Oh, you're John's little brother [sister]. He's such a quality person. We're looking forward to seeing you follow in his footsteps." And then the wheels of competition are set in motion.

Younger siblings have several choices at that point. They can admire their older sibling and do whatever possible to be like (or better yet, surpass) that older sibling. Or, maybe they like living in the reflected glory of a recognized sibling. If not, they may feel more drawn to a less popular brother or sister, since they can then avoid the comparisons. They even may wish they had no siblings at all so they could have all the attention and glory for themselves. Some may go so far as to give up, seeing it as a losing effort. Others may achieve in totally different areas, which then gives them recognition of their own while avoiding the competitive hassle. For some younger siblings, this is a sufficient solution. But for others, the recognition they receive always seems second-rate in their own eyes. In the extreme, some may end up wishing tragedy, such as an accident or even death, on their sibling.

It's also different for an older, achieving sibling to live in the shadow of a younger brother or sister who continues to surpass everything the older sibling has ever done. At one time, recognition was theirs; now, dethronement looms.[8]

Chuck Swindoll describes the effects of jealousy:

No response is more cruel than jealousy. Solomon was right when he said, "Jealousy is cruel as the grave" (Song of Solomon 8:6, *RSV*). Jealousy, if allowed to grow and fester, leads to devastating consequences. If you allow jealousy to rage within your family or between your children, you are asking for trouble. At some point, it will manifest itself in detrimental ways.[9]

"SOS"

In the family with multiple siblings, there is usually one who is more significant than the other—the one with whom there is the most tension, the most connection, the most fear or the most rivalry. He or she is the center of your focus, the one your comparative world revolves around.

This person has the ability to dictate how you feel, whether that be love or inadequacy, success or rejection, worth or anger, discomfort or envy. This is the one you want to outdo, but instead you find yourself experiencing continual defeat at his or her hands. It doesn't take much on that sibling's part to affect you. The others are there, a part of your family system, but it is this special one who has the greatest effect in molding you into the person you are today.

If you had only one sibling in your family, it's easy to identify the special one. If there was more than one sibling, which one sparked the greatest rivalry? Sometimes this rivalry is mutual. In other cases, it's just one-sided, on your part.[10]

In *Mom Loved You Best*, this person is called the "sibling of significance" or SOS. This is what the authors say about the SOS:

"Sibling of significance," or SOS, is a term we have coined to highlight the essential themes of this complex relationship between two people. It combines a sense of danger with the hope of help, the desperation of possible defeat with a feeling of importance, and a desire to come to the rescue when this special person is in trouble. The concept of SOS is an important one to understand because it provides a framework for the exploration of your family dynamics. Although you probably know, if you have two or more siblings, that you don't feel the same way about all of them, you may be most uncomfortable about those unequal feelings. As you examine your relationship with your SOS, you will see that it is absolutely normal and natural to respond differently to each member of your family.

Competitiveness—the fight for superiority over others—is innate to all human beings, especially with siblings of significance and the people who remind you of them. But that doesn't mean the two of you must always be at odds and that you can't be good friends as well as rivals. If you were raised in a functional family, your competitiveness, although it will always be there, is not likely to have become the most important aspect of your relationship with your SOS.

What's more, unless the rivalry has become so intense and out of control that it completely dominates the relationship, having an SOS exerts a positive influence. It provides you with a frame of reference, a way to measure your progress, and one of the few really intimate connections you will ever have. In fact, people who never have a reciprocal SOS—only children or siblings who are the "odd person out" in their families—may well be missing an important developmental ingredient.[11]

You shared memories with this SOS. You have information on him or her—as that SOS does on you—information your parents don't know about. And both of you know how to use it on the other. You probably spent your childhood trying to surpass your SOS in one way or another. You still may be doing this in overt ways or in your mind.

It's interesting to note that, with three children, gender enters into this equation. When one child is the opposite sex of the other two, the contenders are usually those of the same sex.

There is one major problem in rivalry between siblings: There is no winner.

> It is a mistake, sometimes a tragic mistake, to believe you can be better at being your brothers or sisters than they are at being themselves. The truth is, you can only be better at being yourself. In the end, the joy you feel in your own successes comes from "doing your own thing" and accomplishing whatever is important to you, rather than what you think will help you win out over your brother or sister. Think about the Olympic champions who have been most successful when they have measured themselves against their own past performances, their own personal bests, and not those of their competitors. If you choose your goals for yourself and not merely to overpower your SOS, your accomplishments will be much more satisfying. And a lot less hollow.[12]

Did you have a sibling of significance? Do you still have one who qualifies? Was there one who, as a child, was the spoiler of your life, the one you envied? Is there one you can't wait to tell about your success, but from whom you hide your failures? Is there one you would like to impress more than others? Is there one whose disfavor and criticism penetrates and devastates more than others? Is there one sibling you think about more than others? From your perspective, did your parents favor that sibling?

Perhaps you came from a family atmosphere in which rivalry was practically nonexistent. But for many adults, competition was a natural part of growing up. The main question for you to consider is this: Is your life today what you want it to be, or is it being influenced by a sibling in a way that limits you? If your answer is that you have a sibling whose influence is limiting you, then you're letting someone else control your life. Most adults would like to be free from these influences. What about you? What could you do now to move ahead in your life and put your sibling rivalry in the background?

Notes

1. Dr. Ray Guarendi, *Back to the Family* (New York: Villard Books, 1990), p. 227.
2. Joseph Mersand, ed., *Great American Short Biographies* (New York: Dell Publishing Co., 1966), adapted, n.p.
3. Joan Fontaine, *No Bed of Roses* (New York: William Morrow & Company, 1978), pp. 102, 145, 146, 188, adapted.
4. Patti McDermott, *Sisters and Brothers* (Los Angeles: Lowell House, 1992), pp. 105-108, adapted.
5. Marian Sandmaier, *Original Kin* (New York: Dutton, 1994), pp. 84, 85, adapted.
6. Francine Klagsbrun, *Mixed Blessings* (New York: Bantam Books, 1992), p. 13, adapted.
7. John F. McDermott Jr., M.D., *Raising Cain (and Abel Too)* (New York: Wyden Books, distributed by Harper & Row, 1980), p. 16.
8. McDermott, *Raising*, pp. 106-120, adapted.
9. Charles Swindoll, *Joseph* (Nashville: Word Publishing, 1998), pp. 18, 19.
10. Drs. William and Madra Hapworth and Joan Rathner Heilman, *Mom Loved You Best* (New York: Viking Penguin, 1993), pp. 37-41, adapted.
11. Ibid., pp. 42, 43.
12. Ibid., p. 51.

Chapter Six

Other Sibling Relationships

"Double your pleasure, double your fun" are the words in a famous commercial we've listened to and watched for years. This chewing gum ad tries to prove that by chewing their brand, whatever pleasure we experienced before will double. And to catch our attention, who does this company use? Twins—men, women and children of all ages.

Twins: Twice the Fun?

So what about twins? Do twins double the pleasure and fun for a family? Twins have been subjects of conjecture, speculation and study for years. It is special for a family to have twins. You've heard comments like, "That's the family with twin boys," or "They sure will have their hands full with twins!" We identify families by the fact that they have twins. The world seems to love twins (or any multiple births) and gives them an overabundance of attention. The spotlight always seems to be on them.

No matter how much we know about twins, there is still a fascination and a bit of mystery to the special relationship they share. In mythical literature we have the legend of Romulus and Remus, who were supposedly nursed by a she-wolf. In the Scripture we have the conflicted relationship of Jacob and Esau, the twin sons born to Isaac and Rebekah. Children today still read the turn-of-the-century series, The Bobbsey Twins.

The special closeness twins share begins in the womb. Then, while in the crib, they hear one another's sounds, which can be soothing. From birth, they share it all—Mom, Dad, time, attention, nurturing, toys, clothes and food. And they soon become aware not only of the sharing but also of any slight differences between each other. One may be upset because the other crawls, walks and talks earlier. Twins seldom bond with their parents and other family members one at a time. And when people talk about them, it is rarely as individuals but as a pair.

Some parents are delighted to have twins, while others are resentful. Some mothers like the fact that twins keep each other company and entertain one another. There are cases, however, of some twins becoming so inseparably intertwined that they don't bond well with parents or others—even in adulthood. I know one set of twins who developed their own speech patterns and way of communicating with one another as toddlers. Not only did this confuse others, but it also affected the way they talk as adults.

UNAVOIDABLE COMPARISONS

The comparison between siblings is magnified in twins. Starting at birth, every part of their lives is compared: their noses, eyes and ears; the way they speak, play, crawl and walk. Naturally, with fraternal and male/female twins, there may be less comparison than with identical twins. In the latter case, there tends to be more emphasis upon their differences.

When children constantly are compared, it can increase their developmental closeness as well as their own sense of differences and similarities. But this comparison brings a good news/bad news situation. There's always the companionship and even a sense of safety between twins. But it's difficult to develop individuality, especially if parents dress them alike throughout their growing-up years.

It also can be tiring for many twins to live with a lifetime of being compared with one another. Those outside the family often are the ones who tend to see twins as a single unit. Twins dread hearing the familiar question, "How can you tell them apart?" Of course, if they aren't identical, they may hear, "Why don't you look like your brother [sister]?"—a ridiculous question when you think about it, since no one has control over their physical features and attributes.

Although some twins struggle with establishing separate identities, others play the similarites to the hilt. Twins have changed places with one another on dates to see if they could fool the other's interested party. One of my seminary graduate students and his brother often would switch places at work for a day, and they were quite successful in pulling off the deception.

ALIKE, BUT STILL INDIVIDUAL

Even when twins are identical, they have their individual differences. The genetic temperament and personality factors are still evident. One may be brighter or quicker, more perceptive or assertive, or more reserved. Even with twins, there is still a first-born dynamic, if only by a few seconds or minutes. Usually, the firstborn leads. An exception to this is found in the Bible story of Jacob, the second-born twin, who was born hanging onto Esau's heel.

The same dynamics exist between twins as between other siblings. The younger can resent the older, and rivalry can become intense. Sometimes the younger twin says, "I'm the baby of the family, the last born"; or the older says, "I'm three minutes older than my sister." It's more of a symbolic difference for many. Some of the same firstborn sibling expectations—roles and even advantages—can fall on the firstborn twin.

A UNIQUE CLOSENESS?

Is there a special closeness with twins that is absent from other siblings? We've probably all heard stories of twins who have the same thoughts and feelings simultaneously, or who telephone one another at the same time or make corresponding plans without having consulted each other. Is there a special sense or telepathy between them, or is it similar to the closeness and sensitivity that develops in a long-term happy and close marriage? Some say there is an exceptional identification between twins that heightens their sensitivity to one another's moods. This has been referred to as the "twin bond." It's a special emotion established by the close contact and sharing that begins at birth.

Various Twin Relationships

In some cases there is a heightened intuitive sense of one another's thoughts and emotions, which many are at a loss to explain. Do all twins end up with the same or similar relationships? Not really. Dr. Jane Greer has identified four different types of twin relationships.

- The Twins: One type of relationship is simply referred to as "the twins." These two have their lives built around being twins. They perpetuate being identical by being together every possible minute, dressing the same, having the same hairstyle, etc. To them, their identity as twins is more important than who they are as individuals.

- Complementary Twins: In this case, each twin separates the areas of his or her life that complement the other's. They are twins, but they have their own separate areas and agree to keep them separate.
- Indifferent Twins: There twins' identity is based on being different. They couldn't care less about their identity as twins. Separate lives, separate friends and individuality are their calling.
- Sibling Rival Twins: In this relationship, it is all-out competition to see who is better than the other. All aspects of life are fair game, whether social, sports, academic, dating, marriage, career or otherwise. This is where you often end up with a good twin/bad twin combination. If one goes one direction, the other goes the opposite.[1]

Twins and Other Siblings

Twins can have a major impact on other siblings. If a child feels displaced by one new arrival, just imagine the impact of two. When the newest addition turns out to be twins, it's double trouble for the other siblings. Parents can be elated with the two new arrivals, but also exhausted, so there is even less of mom and dad to go around. And twins naturally get more attention, especially from outsiders, which opens the door for potential resentment toward the favored position of twins. If there is just one other sibling in addition to the twins, that one may end up feeling excluded or the "tacked on" child, never able to break into the special twins club.[2,3]

The closeness between twins can complicate the normal transition of separation from other siblings. Twins may go to college together, but when it comes to work and marriage, they're on their own—often for the first time. When one wants to move on with life and the other doesn't, the tension can be extreme. Even with positive moves away from one another, one or both may feel a bit unnerved or even left out in some way. Abandonment can be a big issue when twins transition in different directions. What if one marries young, while the other takes ten more years to take that step? What if a male twin is dating and, after introducing his fiancée to his brother, she falls for him and dumps the first twin? It has happened. Once in a great while twins marry twins, and these matches seem to work well.

It is possible for twins and their siblings to have healthy and special relationships. Parents of twins must exercise wisdom in giving accolades, time and attention to all their children. Whether twins or not, each child needs to develop a healthy individuality. Together or separate, twins have much to offer to others as well as much to receive from them.

Blended Families

Who hasn't heard of the Brady Bunch? For years this reconstituted television family of two attractive parents and six good-looking kids was beamed via television into millions of America's homes. The Bradys were supposed to represent the typical blended family, with a mix of siblings and stepsiblings. But was this portrayal typical of the average stepfamily? Let's look at a cross section of stepfamilies and find out.

Some stepsiblings end up living together full time; for others it can be a part-time situation or even one of seeing each other once or twice a month or less.

Have you ever envisioned what the initial meeting is like between brothers and sisters from stepfamilies? The range of emotions can vary from caution, suspicion, distrust and resentment to curiosity, excitement and anticipation.

> *Research indicates that the relationships that evolve between stepsiblings can have a great effect—either positive or negative—upon a remarriage.*

What occurs between stepsiblings can be just as influential as the ties between biological siblings. Research indicates that the children each partner brings into a stepfamily are often the major source of conflict in this new marriage. The relationships that evolve between stepsiblings can have a great effect—either positive or negative—upon the remarriage.

ADJUSTMENTS

Often the new parent, as well as the stepsiblings, are seen by the other parent's children as intruders. They take away time and attention that used to be theirs exclusively. Stepsiblings feel the pressure of instant intimacy, especially when both parents constantly urge them to get along with each other. There can be power struggles, rivalry and resentment over having to share a room or feeling displaced by the newcomers. While some enjoy the companionship and friendship that develops, others respond as one young boy did: "I didn't ask for an instant brother and sister. I didn't need them, and now I'm stuck with them. I liked my life the way it was."

In a blended family, much is asked of the children. When their own family broke up, they had to adjust to the losses that divorce or abandonment entailed. But with a remarriage, the adjustment is to the additions to the family unit, which can bring a unique set of losses.

Consider the possibilities: In one family, the birth order positions and various roles have been intact for years. Then one day there's a remarriage. One of the first adjustments is the rejuggling of the birth-order positions. A firstborn may no longer own that position because of an older stepsibling, yet both expect to continue to function in that firstborn position. What if the youngest girl was accustomed to being the favorite and the prettiest? Now, a younger version of herself enters the family and upsets her position. What if you end up with two heroes, two caretakers or two scapegoats?

It's common for children to continue to see themselves in their same birth-order positions with their own siblings as well as with the new stepsiblings. Others may be delighted to get an older brother or sister or to have someone of the same gender after having only siblings of the opposite sex. The new stepsiblings may provide diversion or companionship that helps handle the pain of a parental breakup.

Good friendships can develop among stepsiblings, especially during the teen years and on into adulthood. These relationships can start out fresh since they don't have any, or at least not as many, of the childhood issues to carry with them. There's a freedom from old baggage.

NO SHARED HISTORY

This lack of history can also be a problem. There's no emotional depth, no common sharing of years of memories, no intimate connection. Despite this lack—and often a lack of preparation for the blending stepsibling relationships—they are expected to adjust and connect instantaneously. This makes it difficult for them to bond. Just imagine: When the two families join, there's an expectation of instant family life, love, loyalty and sharing. But there are also instant rivalries, resentments and personality clashes. Think of all the sharing that has to occur—bedrooms, dressers, closets, toys, time with parents and family activities. The amount of time the bathroom was available has suddenly been cut in half or less. What makes it worse is when a stepsibling is someone you never would have chosen as a friend.

PART-TIME STEPFAMILIES

When a stepsibling lives elsewhere most of the time, other issues arise. A child may have to give up his or her room to this stepsibling two weekends a month. And what if the standards are different? What if this stepsibling lives in a home where little is expected of the children and they can come and go as they please? The stepsibling may bring this attitude and pattern into a home in which children have to toe the mark and live by strict rules, different values, standards and levels of discipline. This creates tension. There also can be an obvious difference in the standard of living between the two homes. Economic differences between stepfamilies can pit one set of siblings against the other, which in turn can fuel insecurity and conflict.

When stepsiblings come for the weekend, one or both parents may go overboard in catering to their needs and trying to make them feel comfortable in their home away from home. This distracts from the attention usually given to the children who live there permanently. A common complaint is, "Why should I have to share my room, my TV, my mom? She's not their mom. I didn't ask for this."

In stepfamilies, sexual confusions can occur. Sometimes

there is a strong sexual attraction between stepsiblings. The barrier against incest may be lowered since stepbrothers and stepsisters are not blood relatives. It's not unusual for opposite-sex stepsiblings to fight with one another or to become cold and withdrawn in an effort to deal with their sexual feelings. In some cases, as adults, they end up marrying.

A large percentage of families in our society have stepsiblings. Many of them make healthy adjustments. It's a choice, like so many other issues in life.[4,5]

Disabled Siblings

All siblings experience a time when a brother or sister is disabled for a while because of illness. It could be something as temporary as a cold, the flu, measles or a broken leg. It might also be something as life-threatening as cancer or even the dreaded HIV/AIDS. Children react differently to a sick sibling, depending upon their age and closeness of relationship. Siblings can be compassionate, fearful, concerned, sympathetic or even jealous because of the attention the sick child receives.

As adults, most siblings learn to support and console one another. Often it is a sibling who conveys the information and/or bad news about another sibling to the parents. In fact, illness of a sibling at any age can bring with it the potential for greater closeness.

When a sibling is permanently disabled, however, it can change the dynamics of all the relationships.[6] Whenever a family suffers a loss of any kind, including the disability of a child, the siblings are affected, too. They tend to develop a greater than usual level of neediness. They want more nurturing from their parents at a time when their parents have less to give.

If a family has suffered such a loss, the other children may be having a difficult time while the parents' energy is directed toward trying to discover the exact condition of the disabled child. Often the other children struggle with guilt because they are "normal," while their sibling isn't.

When a sibling is handicapped, normal responses—such as anger, jealousy, affection, loyalty—are distorted or intensified. A sister may love her disabled older brother but might even want him dead. She may like the idea of having an older brother but not a handicapped one. Instead of being the protected little sister, she is forced into the role of an older sister. This is a loss for her. And if her brother's handicap came about as the result of an accident or illness rather than as a birth defect, she may feel that something she said, did or even thought or felt might have created the problem.

COMMUNICATION IS A KEY

Too often, when a crisis arises, no one thinks about talking to the other children about what's going on and why. Consequently, they continue to struggle with their feelings, questions and pain. They may feel alone and perhaps quite angry. They may respond in negative and even hurtful ways, especially if they feel neglected.

Then again, parents may not see much of a noticeable change in the nonhandicapped children. Or they may see a very positive change as one child decides to be overly good as a means of survival. This particular child makes few demands on her exhausted and stressed parents and tries to be helpful. But this child, too, has needs that only the parents can meet, and this child may also require an opportunity to grieve.

Many children hide their distress and have to deal with it years later in adulthood. Another common reaction to a suddenly handicapped sibling is for the other children to employ attention-getting mechanisms. It's the only way they know to recapture their parents' attention. And if their attempts are ignored or discounted, they might intensify their efforts by using drugs, running away, setting fires, destroying property and so on. Expressed anger is one way to gain attention.[7]

If the healthy children and the disabled child are similar, there is a higher degree of identification and pain. In addition, the fear of becoming like the disabled brother or sister is intensified, so it's not unusual for healthy siblings to avoid contact or visits to the unhealthy one. And if the disabled sibling was normal and healthy at one time, there is a heightened loss for the other siblings.

Often, the healthy siblings are angry—at their disabled sibling, at parents or at life itself. Having a disabled brother or sister is an inconvenience. The anger may be expressed openly or just ferment internally.

Some children are angry at their parents for having such a child. They could be angry over the time, attention or money directed toward this special child. But anger and jealousy can create guilt.

Some siblings worry about catching the unhealthy child's impairment, especially if it's disease related. They may be afraid of passing the disease on to their own children. They also may worry about who will care for the handicapped sibling if their parents aren't able to do so.

These children worry about the reactions of others to their disabled sibling, wondering what they may be thinking. Do others project the unhealthy sibling's disability or disfigurement onto them?[8]

A common response is embarrassment. Siblings can be embarrassed by the disabled sibling's behavior, noises, way of wailing, being kept at home or sent to a special school. One brother had to drive his retarded sister to school each day because they attended the same high school. But he let her out of the car a block away, so he wouldn't be seen with her by his friends. Many siblings feel an inward tension when they see people making fun of their sibling. They want to protect that sibling but are afraid of others' reactions.[9]

Children raised with a disabled sibling often feel a strong sense of responsibility, either self-imposed or placed there by their parents. Some complain that they feel like miniature parents. Dr. Charlotte Thompson tells the story of a pediatrician who grew up with a disabled sibling. The family knew something was wrong with her brother, but the problem wasn't diagnosed until he was 15. He wasn't expected to do chores or to have outside jobs like the other children. The parents had time and money for him but very little for the others. They put up with temper tantrums and angry explosions from him, but they wouldn't tolerate any expression of anger from the rest of them.

The disabled child knew he was favored and used it to his advantage. He ended up being viewed as the good child and the others as the bad ones.

By the time the problem was diagnosed and a tumor was removed, the family's finances were depleted. During that time, the other children never voiced their concern over the unfairness. When this pediatrician was in counseling for her marriage, her therapist told her,

> You've been carrying your brother on your back all of your life, which is probably one of the reasons you went into pediatrics. You have been trying to understand what happened with your brother and why you always felt him around your neck like a millstone. You have a highly overdeveloped sense of responsibility toward

other children and have tried to mother the world. This has caused emotional problems, marital problems, and has left you feeling drained, angry, and incomplete. Essentially you have had to be your own parent, and after your parents died, you felt a tremendous responsibility for your brother. By transferring his dependence from your parents to you, you created a very difficult problem for yourself. You may well know that people often grow to dislike, or even hate, close individuals on whom they feel dependent. This surely was your brother's case. First he hated your parents, now he hates you.[10]

That situation could have been avoided if the parents had communicated with the other children and they had all worked together as a team. But who helps parents deal with their grief and gives them guidelines for responding to the other children? Usually no one, which is why they and the siblings need the assistance of other parents who have gone through similar struggles.

PARENTS' FEELINGS AND RESPONSES

Parents may be aware that they're not doing what they want or need with the other children. Their grief for the one drains their energy and the emotional investment they want to make in the others. So they feel they're not being the parents they want to be, which adds to their frustration and sense of failure. But during the onset of the crisis with their disabled child, it's unrealistic to think they can carry on family business as usual with the other children. They just don't have enough to give.

The parents' feelings and responses toward all their children will fluctuate as well. They may feel resentment toward the healthy ones or not be as concerned about their well-being. They also may have mixed feelings toward the unhealthy child, even questioning themselves as to whether or not they have grieved enough or have adjusted too soon. Part of their response is anger over the unfairness of what has happened. They may feel they can't invest as much as they want or that they've lost their ability to give. Or they may be afraid to invest too much in the unhealthy child because of the cost to their other children. Another common problem for parents in this situation is that they tend to overreact and overprotect.[11]

HOW SIBLINGS ARE AFFECTED

Note what research has said about the impact on siblings of disabled children:

- Older siblings adjust better than younger children to having a brother or sister with disabilities, with the exception of the eldest daughter, who doesn't adjust as well.
- Eldest daughters often are given the task of caring for the child with special needs, much more often than are any other children in the family.
- Children are more affected by having a sibling with a disability if that sibling is of the same gender.
- If there are only two children in the family, and if the nondisabled sibling is a girl, she suffers more adverse effects.
- If there are only two children in the family, and one has a disability, the other is more pressured to fulfill the parents' hopes and dreams for success in their children. If the nondisabled child is a girl, she is also assigned more caregiving responsibility.
- Siblings of children with disabilities tend to show positive qualities of being well adjusted, mature beyond

their years, tolerant of differences in people, helpful toward people, and aware of social needs.

- Siblings can be excellent teachers of their brothers and sisters with disabilities because they are in a different position in the family.
- Siblings may judge the worth of their friends by the friends' reactions to their brother or sister with the disability.
- The siblings may feel pressure to overachieve.
- Siblings may overidentify with a mildly disabled brother or sister or may, as they reach teen years, not consider a severely disabled sibling a person.
- Siblings may feel that requests by parents for help with the brother or sister with a disability are an intrusion on their time, or they may view it as a privilege to cooperate with parents.[12]

It's interesting that choosing a helping profession—doctor, nurse, physical therapist, social worker, counselor—as a vocation is common among the siblings of disabled people. Possibly one reason for this may be that some of these children carry guilt, feelings of responsibility or a sense of chronic sorrow or sadness into adulthood. Sometimes the acceptance of a disabled brother or sister gets harder as the kids grow older. As a daughter of some friends put it,

> I grow older and change. But my sister stays the same, and at times it seems as though she goes backward. She's an adult like I am, but I'm a real adult, and she's still in infancy. And she always will be. That's sad.

Siblings face numerous pressures that we don't even think about. For instance, what does a child say to others when asked about an older sister who is on drugs and has just become pregnant? Or when a sibling who doesn't look disabled in any way is nonverbal and can't answer for himself or herself?

Sometimes the less severe the impairment, the more difficult it is for the siblings, since they may feel embarrassed about their brother's or sister's behavior. If the impairment were more severe, it would be self-explanatory.

OUR EXPERIENCE

Our second child was a profoundly mentally retarded boy. He died at 22, and his mental ability was that of an 18-month-old. We wondered how Matthew affected our daughter, Sheryl. She seemed to handle his presence all right, but we weren't always sure. We remembered various incidents over the years. One day when Matthew was very young, Sheryl was at a neighbor's house where they had a baby three months younger than Matthew. That baby was turning over and sitting up. Sheryl came home and asked why their baby was able to do those things and Matthew wasn't, even though he was older. When my wife, Joyce, told her that Matthew was slower and wouldn't be able to do those things for a while, Sheryl didn't say anything, but the hurt was visible on her face.

As Sheryl grew older, she never hid from the fact that her brother was mentally retarded. She never shielded it from her friends. We wondered if she would be embarrassed about it, but she would bring her friends home and when they met Matthew she would say, "This is my brother, Matthew. He's retarded." Then she would go on with what she was doing. Her friends were the ones who didn't seem to know how to respond.

As Sheryl moved through junior and senior high school, we noticed that she seemed to be sensitive to the needs of other retarded people, as well as protective of them if others mistreated them. When Sheryl was in her early thirties, I asked her how Matthew had affected her and what problems she experienced in having a disabled brother.

"I don't think of any problems I had with Matthew being retarded when I was young," she said. "I didn't feel left out in any way. In fact, my first memory of Matthew was when Grandma and I were taking him for a stroll around the block and he had a seizure. Grandma became very upset. I went to a house, knocked on the door, told the lady that my brother was having a seizure and asked to borrow a spoon. The lady and I held him and used the spoon in his mouth so he wouldn't choke. I wasn't upset. It made me feel like I was really a part of the family since I could help him.

"When I was young, his condition didn't bother me. It was like riding in an airplane or going through an earthquake when I was a child. I didn't fully understand the significance and all the ramifications of those situations, nor of retardation. When I became an adult I understood, and then it was difficult to deal with. I couldn't handle going to Matthew's home and seeing all the other disabled children. It just tore me to pieces. I have a difficult time seeing retarded children now."

After Sheryl said that, we talked a bit more. I told her that I understood and that I have a similar response and sensitivity to seeing anyone with a disability. It took me years to discover that what I was feeling was the wish that I could reach out and heal that person—make him or her whole—followed by the frustration of knowing I couldn't.

Sheryl floored me with her response: "I don't think Matthew's retardation was something for us to try to heal. I think his purpose was to bring healing to all of us. We're all different because of him. I know I'm a different person because of Matthew."

I just stood there, letting the truth of her profound statement sink in. Her words left me speechless. My tears were the only response. When she came across the room to hug me, I told her that was one of the most special things she had ever said.

Yes, it can be difficult with a disabled sibling. But it can also be one of life's greatest opportunities to learn compassion as well as to experience God's comfort.

MUCH DEPENDS ON ATTITUDE

When parents die, who becomes responsible or cares for the disabled sibling? Custody and responsibility are major concerns. There may be a strong resistance to taking on this responsibility, and sibling squabbles have erupted over who is to do what. Often the other siblings have their own families by this time, and it's difficult to become too involved. Sometimes, if one adult sibling hasn't married yet, the others feel it's this sibling's responsibility, since he or she doesn't have the same responsibilities as the rest of them.

Living with a disabled sibling is not all negative for the brothers and sisters. As Sheryl so aptly expressed it, the disabled person can bring joy and meaning into the lives of others. So much depends on what attitude us developed toward the disabled sibling.

Notes

1. Dr. Jane Greer with Edward Myers, *Adult Sibling Rivalry* (New York: Crown Publishing, 1992), pp. 189-96, adapted.
2. Helene S. Arnstein, *Brothers and Sisters/Sisters and Brothers* (New York: E.P. Dutton, 1979), pp. 126-41, adapted.
3. Greer and Myers, *Adult,* pp. 185-98, adapted.

4. Francine Klagsbrun, *Mixed Feelings* (New York: Bantam Books, 1992), pp. 128, 136-39, 142-45, adapted.
5. Arnstein, *Brothers/Sisters,* pp. 156-66, adapted.
6. Klagsbrun, *Mixed,* pp. 232-34, adapted.
7. Charlotte E. Thompson, *Raising a Handicapped Child* (New York: Morrow, 1986), pp. 62-64, adapted.
8. Helen Featherstone, *A Difference in the Family* (New York: Penguin Books, 1980), pp. 142-71, adapted.
9. Klagsbrun, *Mixed,* pp. 235-37, adapted.
10. Thompson, *Handicapped,* p. 66.
11. Therese A. Rando, *Grieving* (Lexington, Mass.: Lexington Books, 1988), pp. 178, 179, adapted.
12. Thomas M. Skric, Jean Ann Summers, Mary Jane Brotherson, and Ann P. Turnbull, "Severely Handicapped Children and Their Brothers and Sisters," *Severely Handicapped Young Children and Their Families,"* ed. Jan Blacker (Orlando: Academic Press, 1984), pp. 215-46.

Chapter Seven

The Battles of Siblings

Over the years I have seen numerous wars, not so much between nations or between parents and children, but ongoing wars between siblings. Some of these wars have lasted for over a quarter of a century. The weapons used include bickering, hateful comments, spiteful letters, hung-up phone calls, not talking or seeing one another for years and even permanent separation. Siblings lose one another in death, but in some ways it's worse when the loss is by conflict.

Sibling Battles: Helping You to Be All You Can Be

All siblings disagree, fight and compete as children. You probably did. What were your fights about? Was it to gain power and control over a brother or sister? Could it have been a desire to have more attention or a better position with your parents? Or perhaps it was over territory, toys, other possessions, friends or a desire to goad your brother or sister into a reaction. Were these fights always negative and harmful? Probably not. They had a purpose, part of which was to educate and prepare you for life.

Even though the battles were painful at times, they helped you come to understand your own strengths and limitations. You learned to assess your ability to bargain, negotiate or handle conflict and anger, all of which you would need as you grew older. You possibly found out about loyalty, fairness and trust. You learned that it was all right to disagree, to have different points of view, that as different as you and your sibling are, it's all right for you to be you and for them to be whoever they are. And, hopefully, you learned how to resolve differences, so you could respond differently the next time. You may not have liked the hassling, but having experienced it, you are better off and better prepared for life than those who grew up without it. This experience helped you to relate and connect better in your adult world.

When you disagree with a sibling, as compared to a friend, you probably are more blunt and honest. You usually don't hold back. Why? Because you feel more secure with family members than with friends. The relationship has a greater sense of permanency, despite differences. Therefore, the risk involved in expressing yourself honestly is lessened.

When the Hatchet Is Never Buried

The fighting and squabbling of childhood normally diminishes in adulthood—at least, for most it does. For others, the ongoing battle continues. It may be a continuation of the same issues of childhood, or it could be the same themes but with different packaging. Almost every phone call or get-together can become a continuation of where the last phone call or visit left off, without a break since childhood. A 40-year-old mother told me,

I talk to my younger sister every second and fourth Sunday of the month. It's the only way it works for my own husband and children. They leave the house for several hours, since they know the outcome of our phone conversation. It won't go well. It's never gone well. It probably will never go well between us. I'm in a terrible mood after the phone call, and I don't blame my family for not wanting to be around to catch the fallout. When we talk on the phone, it's as though we had just talked five minutes ago. We pick up the arguing right where we left off. It'd be nice to get along—I guess. I'm not sure I know what that would be like.

What are the issues over which adult siblings clash? What keeps them standing face-to-face, at odds with one another, rather than arm in arm, side by side, supporting each other? Are these new issues or repetitive remnants?

For many it's a parental contribution—the old nemesis of favoritism. Closely aligned with this is the scapegoating of one child. It's interesting to see that the "good child" in the eyes of the parent becomes the bad one in the eyes of the scapegoat. As adults, scapegoats often want the scales balanced for what they tolerated as they grew up. It's payback time. But all too often, what the scapegoat considers fair and equitable retribution has no end to it. The scapegoat resents one or all of the siblings because of the disfavored position he or she had to endure, while the other siblings resent what is occurring now.

Another way parents keep the squabbling alive is when one, either unwittingly or purposely, pits one child against another. Perhaps it's the mother who calls the other siblings to let them know about one sibling's new green BMW, the latest promotion, the grades of a particular grandchild (with the seeming insinuation that the other grandchildren aren't as bright), or the privileged sibling's trip to Europe that the others can't afford.

There's also the parent who puts a damper on the excitement you feel over an experience or attainment by downplaying it in comparison to another sibling's accomplishment. Fred told me,

> Dad's a real piece of work in this arena. I'll call him about something we buy, and I know his first words will be, "What did you pay for it?" And when I tell him, he'll say my brother or sister bought one of those and either say it's no good and I should have talked to him or her first, or he or she paid less and got a better deal than I did. It's like he wants us at odds with each other. I don't understand why he's always doing this.

Perhaps, even in adulthood, a parent has more control over the siblings when they're at one another's throats.

I've seen children of all ages—from 8 to 88—argue and fight. What and how they do this is a mirror image of their parents' pattern of not getting along. The parents were the role models for this negative behavior.

But parents aren't the only cause for sibling conflicts. Siblings themselves can be the problem. Sometimes you inherit a sibling you just don't get along with. As one said, "What did I ever do to deserve this sister? Someone up there must not like me very much." You end up wishing you had been cut out of the will or disinherited rather than having to put up with a particular sibling.

Different temperaments or personality types can clash. One sibling may even be mean and cruel to the others. I've seen one sibling in a family whose life's calling seemed to be to make life miserable for everyone else. In another family, two of the children were so competitive (by their own doing) they ended up hating each other. In other families, an older and younger sibling may clash because the older one tends to be bossy and controlling with the younger. The younger ends up feeling as if he or she is being babied, while the older resents the added responsibility, even if it is self-imposed.

Billy Tried to Get His Goat

Fighting can take many forms and expressions. Sometimes a sibling will tolerate the abuse and embarrassment from another sibling. I remember one particular case where it was an older brother who was the tolerant one. Jimmy had a brother named Billy who was 14 years younger. In many ways, they were more like strangers than brothers.

When Billy was 8, Jimmy already was preparing to graduate from the U.S. Naval Academy. By the time Billy was 15, their father became very ill. As a result, Billy ended up staying on the farm to care for his dying father. When the father died, Jimmy inherited the farm and Billy got a lump sum of cash, which he went through very quickly. When the money was gone, Billy asked Jimmy for a job at the farm warehouse. Jimmy obliged, with the understanding that Billy would be treated the same as any of the other employees. Eventually, Billy went into the Marines and then on to the University of Georgia. Unfortunately, he flunked out.

When Billy's older brother became the governor of Georgia, Billy was given the chance to run the family farm; both he and the business did well. But then reversals came. His older brother, Jimmy Carter, was elected president of the United States. Jimmy then put the business in a blind trust to avoid a conflict of interest. Billy tried to buy the business, but the offer was refused. Billy had no job and, in a sense, no identity. He felt as if his life was over. Resentment began to build toward his brother, whom he considered responsible for his problems. This resentment came out in behavior that embarrassed the president. President Carter's advisors always were concerned that Billy might create problems. Previous presidents like Lyndon Johnson and Richard Nixon had to take steps to keep their brothers out of the limelight, but President Carter did not.

Over the next four years, Billy made the headlines numerous times. He showed up drunk at news gatherings and social functions. When the president needed to retain Jewish loyalties for his second term, Billy made anti-Semitic comments. Billy received a large amount of money for a questionable sale, was hospitalized for alcohol abuse and was threatened with foreclosure on his $300,000 home. The president was caught in a good brother/bad brother bind. But he didn't publicly chastise Billy or try to contain him. He was silent about his brother, even though inside he probably carried a painful concern.

Many siblings can be locked into mutual misery. This pattern was probably nothing new for Jimmy and Billy. Each had his own lifestyle and identity. It's as though the actions of each one affirmed the identity of the other. As you look at these well-known brothers in contrast to each other, their chosen lifestyles come to the forefront. President Carter's Christian beliefs, as well as his sense of values and morality, are much more prominent when contrasted to Billy's escapades.[1]

Perhaps Billy's lifestyle is a classic example of the sibling who, in an effort to gain attention—even if it's negative—always seems to end up in trouble. For some, it's a way of trying to "make contact." It's not unusual for some siblings to make contact with one another in the only way they know how—differing, fighting, bickering, quarreling. For them, it seems better than no contact at all. That sort of negative behavior gets carried over into adult attempts to make contact with others, because it reminds them of their family connection.

Conflicts Caused by Crisis

Many siblings get along quite well most of the time, as long as everything is peaceful and calm. But let some type of crisis or transition occur, and everything cuts loose. Any crisis can bring a shift in attitudes, balance of relationships and behavior. Moving away from home to work or attend school, getting married, having trouble with the law, getting pregnant or getting someone pregnant outside of wedlock, feeling abandoned by someone who was close for years, getting a new in-law who doesn't "fit" with existing family members—any or all of these things can cause major problems.[2]

One such event, which really isn't a crisis event but can be turned into one, is holiday gatherings. For instance, take Thanksgiving or Christmas. These holidays can be times of fun and deep satisfaction, but they can have their dark side, too. Although festive, delightful, memorable events for some, for others they can become replays of historical wars, including all the skirmishes and battles. Consider the possibilities. You all gather together for Christmas and . . .

- Who sits where at the table? Do you sit in order of importance or according to your role or pecking order when you grew up?
- What about the gifts? Do you sit and mentally assess the price of your gift as well as the gifts given to siblings? Does this activate memories?
- Do your parents show as much appreciation for the gift you gave them as the ones they received from your

siblings? Are there any nonverbal messages floating throughout the room because someone feels slighted?

- Are any of the grandchildren being slighted compared to the attention being given to the other grandkids? Everyone wants his or her children to get their fair share of everything.
- Perhaps the holiday gatherings of your childhood were positive and wonderful. The gatherings now, however, are filled with tension and hassles. There are three times as many people. One sibling's spouse dominates the conversation, another comes in half drunk, one sibling would rather be elsewhere and two are glued to the tube.
- It could be you're not getting as much attention as your spouse and you feel you're being replaced in your family's affections.

How do you settle who gets to host the next holiday gathering? It could be that several want it in their homes, or perhaps everyone has an excuse, so they look to you since "You have a bigger place. And it's older, so we can't do much damage to it."

You see, family get-togethers are musts for most families. And it's expected that everyone will attend. These events can be stressful because they bring together those who may prefer avoiding one another. This could include parents or siblings or both. How do you handle a family gathering in which the wife of one sibling divorced her husband and married his brother—and to top it off, she has children from both marriages?

Some family gatherings include birthdays, Thanksgiving, Christmas, Fourth of July, etc. These are times when conflicts and hurts can be carried over from the previous get-together, such as someone having been insulted over the food, giving an inappropriate gift or one sibling's kids being obnoxious and rude.

Most of us have high hopes and expectations for the holidays, but they may not work out that way. Perhaps your past and present clash. You've changed the role your family placed upon you, and now they pressure you to return to the familiar role. If you find yourself slipping back into that role, you're upset at yourself, questioning whether you ever really changed that role in the first place.[3]

Caring for Parents

Another potential for conflict is the role reversal children must experience, whether they want to or not. As your parents age and begin to slow down or experience the effects of illness and/or aging, you may end up becoming a parent to your parent. Children begin to take responsibility for the parent's care, which could include doctors' appointments, medicines, where the

> *A potential for conflict is the role reversal children must experience. As your parents age and begin to slow down or experience the effects of illness, you may end up becoming a parent to your parent.*

parent lives, transportation. Which sibling takes charge, and why? Will everyone pitch in and do their share? Does the sibling who bailed out of his responsibilities as a child do the same now? Does one sibling take charge and make decisions without consulting the others, or are the others glad not to be involved?

It's not uncommon at a time like this to hear statements like, "You were Dad's favorite. Now it's up to you. It's payback time"; or "You're the oldest. This responsibility comes with all the privileges you got." You may have one sibling who volunteers for the caregiving in the belief that this act will find favor with the parents and may influence a change in the will. Unfortunately, the care of a parent can be the playing field for competition. In the book *You and Your Aging Parents,* the authors say,

> A highly competitive group of brothers and sisters may continue to compete later in life, although not quite as directly with each other. But when their mother begins to age, they may resume open competition with each other over her welfare, particularly if she was the original source of their competitiveness. Each sibling may claim to be considering Mother's well-being, but the underlying motivation is winning out in a final family contest.[4]

Unfortunately, an inequity often exists in caring for parents. Practically every study indicates it's the daughter (and sometimes the daughter-in-law) who bears the responsibility of being the caregiver, although it's not always the eldest who has that responsibility. I was shocked when I discovered this next finding: A mother spends about 17 years caring for a dependent child, but because of the increase of life expectancy today, this same woman could spend 18 years helping elderly parents! There doesn't seem to be a break for her. Aging parents need to be cared for and often expect it. What happens when the brothers fail to help, giving a typical male response of offering advice and criticism from the sidelines? Anger and tension result, which isn't helpful to caregiving duties.

Are your parents living? Who will assist in their caregiving when the time arrives? Has this been discussed? Have plans been made for their care? If not, perhaps that's an issue you need to address with your siblings right now.

Where There's a Will, There's a Fray

One other issue that needs to be addressed is money. Sometimes children begin thinking about their parents' money and possessions and what will come to them, years before their parents' demise. They lay claim to what they think is rightly theirs beforehand, and even then begin to guard it jealously. Some even have the audacity to ask for their share of the inheritance beforehand. But that's not new, is it? Jesus told about it in a parable:

> There was a man who had two sons. The younger one said to his father, "Father, give me my share of the estate." So he divided his property between them (Luke 15:11,12).

This son asked his father for his inheritance while his father was alive and well. In traditional Middle Eastern culture this means, "Father, I am eager for you to die!" This is an outrageous request, an unthinkable one in that culture. Today, though, there are many children who drain their parents in more subtle ways. They borrow money from their parents, promising to pay it back, which rarely happens. That angers the other children, for they perceive this as hurting their parents and perhaps cutting into their own inheritance.

In Jesus' story, the father granted the request, which meant that he gave to his son a third of all he owned, the usual amount of inheritance given to the youngest child. But the father couldn't go down to the local bank and draw that out. He had most of it in possessions, which had to be divided and then sold. *The New English Bible* says of the prodigal that he "turned the whole of his share into cash" (Luke 15:13). All of what happened was known by the community, and it was a source of shame.

Today, it is the contesting of wills in court and family fights reported in the newspapers that are a source of shame. In Jesus' time, the Jewish laws provided for the division of an inheritance (when the father was ready to do so), but did not grant the children the right to sell until after the father's death. It seems that not much has changed in families and children's desires over the centuries.[5]

What did money mean in your family of origin? Was it sparse or plentiful? Was it distributed fairly, or was it tied up in favoritism? Did your family grow upward or downward financially? Were possessions or money ever used as bribes, rewards or punishment?

Children often equate money or possessions with love:

- If you're good in the store, I'll buy you a treat.
- If you get an A, I'll give you ten dollars.
- If you get straight A's, we'll pay for your college. If you don't, you're on your own.

Did you ever have your allowance taken away for being bad? One author says,

> The use of money to stimulate performance arouses a variety of feelings in the child. The money he receives assumes unwarranted magnitude since it symbolizes parental acceptance or rejection. It stimulates sibling rivalry and develops demanding attitudes in the child, as he struggles to be the most favored one. He may use it negatively in the relationship with his brothers and sisters to bolster him in his rivalries with them.[6]

When parents die, the living trust or will can be a family time bomb. It can reopen old wounds and create new ones. Wills divide money and families. Some siblings never stop their wrangling over the possessions. When parents die, one way of knowing and remembering them is through their possessions. This also can represent a holding on to the past. If the family has had a positive relationship, siblings are able to handle what others would perceive as inequities. If the family relationships were negative, everything may be seen as an inequity. What a child is given through a will is more than the money or possessions. It is a message to them about their worth in their parents' eyes. It's like a parental stamp of approval.

Especially difficult for siblings to handle is favoritism from an inheritance, since their own emotional state at the time of a parent's death is somewhat fragile. They're in the midst of grief, trying to handle their loss. What happens because of the will may constitute another loss. Frequently, at that point, siblings begin to fight or sever relationships, not because of what another sibling has done but because of what a parent has done. Parents often fail to remember that an inheritance says something about the relationship between them and their children. What happens after a parent dies is an extension of what happened between parents and children during life. You've probably seen portrayals of the reading of a will on TV or in the movies. The attorney is present, along with all the survivors, sitting there with somewhat stoic, expressionless faces, trying not to betray their inner feelings. Inside, each person is wondering what he or she will receive and if it will be fair. In some readings of a will, turmoil erupts, as well as intense, angry reactions, as expectations are destroyed. Then the war begins—again.

Commodore Vanderbilt is a famous name in our country. When he died in 1878, he left more than $100 million, tax-free.

But because his children did not please him equally, he left them unequal portions. Five daughters were given only $250,000 each, while three others were given slightly larger but unequal amounts, and these were all in trust. His youngest son, Cornelius Jr., who was a womanizer and gambler, was given even less, and then only if his behavior was "exemplary." The favorite son, William, who was responsible and a moneymaker, was given the rest of the estate. Two sisters and Cornelius Jr., contested the will, and there was a scandal. Eventually, there were some small adjustments.

> *If you have a long-term difficulty involving either a sister or brother, perhaps a new level of expectation and a new way of thinking would help.*

Joan Crawford, a famous movie actress, adopted four children—Christina, Christopher, Cathy and Cynthia. She abused Christopher and Christina. Eventually, the children rebelled, with Christopher running away from home several times as a child and Christina defying her mother. In her will, Joan gave her personal property "to the nearest and most attentive" of her daughters, Cathy. To Cathy and Cindy she left $77,500 each. She also left gifts to others as well as to charities. But to her two eldest she said, "It is my intention to make no provision herein for my son, Christopher, or my daughter Christina, for reasons which are well known to them."[7]

Changing Expectations

If you have a long-term difficulty involving either a sister or brother, perhaps a new level of expectation and a new way of thinking would help. With which sibling do you struggle most? Identify that sibling by name, and then make a list of his or her specific behaviors or responses that bother you the most.

1. _____

2. _____

3. _____

4. _____

Consider what one step you could take to help yourself accept the fact that this sibling has these negative or aggravating traits. One man formulated a specific statement to help him accept his sibling's character defects:

> My older brother is critical of me. I recognize that, and I'm fairly comfortable with it being this way. I'm coming to realize that this is his cover or protection against some hurt or defeat in his life. I don't understand why. I may know someday; then again, I may not. Right now, at least, I can't expect any more than this.

Perhaps the most likely way to effect a change is to pray specifically for this individual. Ask God to give you a heightened degree of understanding, patience and acceptance for him or her, especially for the traits or responses you don't like. Ask God to do a healing work at the very root of these problems.

One counselee told me an amazing story. Not every situation will turn out this well, but many do.

> The last time I saw my older sister—the family perfectionist and scorekeeper of the faults of others—I simply told her that it was perfectly all right for her to attempt to be perfect and expect us to be that way. It was also all right for her to point out our faults, and we would accept her doing this. But I also said that I was concerned about her, because if she was this way toward us, she was probably the same way toward herself. I told her I would be praying for her that the Lord would help her discover the root cause of her being so hard on herself.
>
> I concluded by saying that I was more concerned about her way of treating herself than the rest of us. She didn't say anything, and I thought she was going to cry. She called yesterday, and it was like talking to a stranger. She wasn't critical; she was actually friendly. I can't believe the change.

A family member's negative characteristics often assume such a prominent position in our thinking that they soon overshadow the positive traits. Sometimes we need to get another person's perspective or interpretation of an encounter with the difficult person. A more objective observer may be able to help us identify the positives, as well as reinterpret those things that always have appeared as negatives.

Take a minute now to identify some of the positive characteristics of the sibling you find most difficult. Ask for input from someone else if you have difficulty doing so. Write down four of the person's positive qualities in the spaces provided. It may even help to let the person know that you are aware of these positive traits in his or her life.

1. _____

2. _____

3. _____

4. _____

Notes

1. Stephen Bank and Michael D. Kahn, *The Sibling Bond* (New York: Basic Books, 1982), pp. 229, 230, adapted.
2. Francine Klagsbrun, *Mixed Feelings* (New York: Bantam Books, 1992), pp. 255-66, adapted.
3. Dr. Jane Greer with Edward Myers, *Adult Sibling Rivalry* (New York: Crown Publishing, 1992), pp. 138-40, adapted.
4. Barbara Silverstone and Helen Kandel Hyman, *You and Your Aging Parents* (New York: Pantheon Books, 1976), p. 43.
5. Kenneth E. Bailey, "The Pursuing Father," *Christianity Today*, (26 October 1968), p. 35, adapted.
6. Francis Loman Feldman, *The Family in a Money World* (New York: Family Service Association of America, 1957), p. 44.
7. Bob Thomas, *Joan Crawford, A Biography* (New York: Simon & Schuster, 1978), p. 267.

Chapter Eight

The Survival Tactics We Use

Perhaps you've heard the phrase, "The best defense is a good offense." In sports, coaches emphasize both defense and offense. You can have a good offense, but without a good defense you can still lose. The same is true in war. Countries have to have a good defense system. Some of our best fighter planes are loaded with defensive devices to ward off incoming missiles from the enemy.

Sibling Survival Systems

In a family, each member develops his or her own safety or protective system, an attempt to survive and not come out a loser. It's a way of trying to control what goes on within the family system that otherwise might be overwhelming. It helps family members to know they can survive and that they're just as competent as others. Most people develop their own defensive weapon system, as well as their arsenal of offensive weapons.

Siblings are no different. Most develop and refine their survival systems through interaction with their brothers and sisters. Even when they have good relationships and get along most of the time, they have their arsenals available when needed. When a sibling is threatened, feels insecure, feels inferior or is afraid he or she is going to lose, then the walls go up and countermeasures are developed. Sometimes we call these "coping skills."

Siblings can be your greatest support, but they can also trigger your negative responses quicker and better than anyone else. The trigger can be as simple as something they say, how they say it, what they don't say, what they do, don't do or say they will do. Do you ever really win or lose with a sibling? Perhaps not. It's like an ongoing sparring match to which the combatants return now and then.

In the previous chapter we talked about the various things siblings battle over. Now we need to identify the tactics, or protective responses, they use with one another. These tactics are learned in their family and often are employed in the workplace as well as within their own marriages and family life. They may use various tactical maneuvers, even though they probably settle on one or two that work better than the others.

As you consider these tactics, you also need to consider several questions about their presence in your life. Are these helping or hindering your relationships with others? Have you chosen these responses out of your own free will, or are they there because of the influence of your siblings? In other words, are they controlling you by eliciting these responses from you, rather than you controlling them? Are these responses in line with Scripture? Are there better ways to respond, according to God's Word?

Let's consider how siblings learn to interact with one another. As you read, ask yourself, "Is this tactic used in my relationship with my sibling? If so, is it used regularly? Is it a pattern? Is there a better way to respond?"

REJECTION

Rejection is a good protective device against anyone who appears to be a threat. When you're under attack, you can ignore or reject your sibling or what they say. Some are able to reject the attacks outwardly, but it still hurts internally. Others have such a good rejection system that nothing penetrates. Older siblings are more likely to employ this tactic if they were dethroned by a younger sibling. Rejection usually is based on the pecking order. It works well for some if they have to deal with an overbearing sibling. When rejection is used, it sends the message, "It's all right for you to say or do what you're doing. I can handle it. It won't affect me."

But there's another side to rejection. Do you use it as an offensive tactic? If so, how does this build your relationship? Does it resolve problems, draw you closer or fracture your relationship?

THE BABY APPROACH

Some use the baby approach. When attacked, they regress and respond in helplessness. It gets others to back off and may even get them to step in to protect the "baby." If they appear helpless and defenseless, they send out the message, "Rescue me," and someone usually does. If they can't take care of themselves, someone else needs to pick up the slack. They gain attention, freedom from responsibility and, above all, control. If no one helps them, who ends up looking bad? You or them?

INFANTILIZATION

Some use infantilization tactics, which are a means of making someone else feel and act like a baby. Anyone can employ this type of tactic, but usually older ones like it because it makes others feel incompetent. Those who use this tactic often make statements like the following:

- I'll take care of this. That way it will be done right.
- Of course I'm the executor of the will. I've been around longer.
- We'll have Christmas at our place again. We know what everyone needs, and we want the day to go smoothly.

Infantilization is a painful technique, one that can make others feel inadequate or even stupid, crushing their spirit and creativity. Too often the person on the receiving end begins to buy into what is being said. Making another feel incompetent and childlike goes counter to the biblical pattern of relating.

GUILT

Another approach, or tactic, is guilt, which can be effective, especially if those on the receiving end see themselves as being good or being conformers—those who follow the rules. If someone says or does something to make them feel bad or guilty, they wonder, What did I do wrong? Did I overdo or not do enough? They get hurt because they feel they have failed.

But guilt works. It may work for you, too. If you use guilt on siblings, you may end up feeling superior to them. I've seen people use guilt on spouses, siblings, children and even dogs. It works—and it hurts. But it's not the best way to relate to others. We're neither called to be guilt collectors nor guilt activators.

ILLNESS

Some use illness as their offense or defense mechanism. They "milk" their real illness for all it's worth or else create an illness.

It's another way of controlling, and it usually works. Using illness to control others is a great passive-aggressive technique. Some have actual symptoms, but they accentuate them. If they want help and assistance, they get it, usually without even asking. They don't have to risk failure. They don't have to put out much personal effort. And they can feel good about others helping and taking on extra work because, after all, they're sick and the others aren't.

If you allow yourself to be victimized by this sort of tactic, you end up not only with your own responsibilities but also someone else's. The challenge then becomes, how do you live your life without being overwhelmed by another's? You don't get much attention, but the other person gets a lot. On top of that, you find yourself struggling with the conflicting emotions of resentment, responsibility and compassion.[1]

MARTYRDOM

The tactical preference of some siblings is martyrdom. Their self-pity is like an infection. No matter what happens, it overwhelms and crushes them. They give off the very air of defeat. They are passive and helpless, and they brood over insignificant issues. To control others, they refuse their offers of help, choosing instead to wallow in their self-affliction. If you are the object of martyr tactics, you end up feeling at least as terrible as the martyr. But if you don't jump in to help, who gets blamed? Most siblings have a desire to help brighten up the martyr's day, but their offers usually are rebuffed.

Martyrs can wreak havoc on family gatherings. They tend to "bleed" on everyone else. Their favorite answer when challenged to cheer up is "I can't." Do you know why martyrs refuse your help? They actually may feel anxiety if they experience pleasure and security. Instead of feeling better when things go well, they feel worse. They're afraid of losing control. Their attitude does not portray self-sufficiency but rather self-sacrifice.

Martyrs are gifted in inducing guilt in others. But the reality is that you never can do enough for martyrs. They can drain you of your energy. It is impossible to solve their problems with advice. The only thing you can do, either personally or in conjunction with other family members, is to perform some sort of an intervention, a direct confrontation of the situation, in an attempt to force the martyr to face the truth. In addition, you can ask the martyr not to share misfortunes at family gatherings. Finally, suggest that for every negative, he or she should share two positives. This method may not solve the problem, but it does send a clear message.[2]

BULLYING

Another approach is the override. Siblings who use this tactic are very open about their style. They probably cut their first teeth on the book *How to Win by Intimidation*. In school we called them bullies. They didn't drive a car, they drove a steamroller. These siblings may be older, more favored than others or even smarter. Perhaps when they were young they were given more power and authority by a parent, and they never relinquished it. Intimidation is responsible for sexual, physical and emotional sibling abuse. Any sibling who appears weak is a target for this type of individual. Often it takes the combined strength of several siblings to wrestle the power and influence away from this person.

BLAMING

I've seen a number of siblings who have perfected another tactic, the art of blaming. They do it directly and indirectly. The slightest weakness or failure on the part of other siblings is all the fuel blamers need to indict them. They serve as accuser, prosecutor, jury and judge. It's a great tactic for redirecting attention away from their own failures. Blamers are like mountains of stone in the way they hold on to their positions. They don't budge. They're like bulldogs hanging on to the blame, so they can hit other siblings with it again and again.

You may have heard of history revisionists, those who rewrite history to fit their own viewpoints and feed their own agendas. That's what blamers try to do—change history for their own benefit. Blamers are on the lookout for victims, and they usually wait to pounce until others are around to confront.[3]

VOLCANOES

There's an interesting passage in the book of Proverbs, which says, "Make no friendship with a man given to anger, nor go with a wrathful man, lest you learn his ways" (22:24,25, *RSV*). This Scripture describes a hothead, one who blows up at the slightest provocation. I like the description given by author Les Parrott III, who calls this kind of person a volcano. As children, these volcanoes were the family time bombs, ready to go off at a moment's notice. These siblings are similar to old-fashioned locomotives that never shut down. The fire in the engine was always left burning so that, when necessary, the engineer could get up a head of steam quickly. The volcano types constantly are building up steam, always ready to erupt. And anyone can be the target of their wrath. Worse yet, you never know when they'll erupt. They're cynical, and they question others' statements and motives. They have the "gift" of faultfinding. Trust is very difficult for them. They're rude and even offensive. Their bumper stickers could read, "I get mad—and I get even." They retaliate and seek revenge. They have scores to settle. It is a pattern that begins in childhood and usually continues into adulthood.

Volcanoes use anger as their defense against painful relationships. Deep down, they may want the rest of the siblings to come close, but their behavior pushes others away. Who wants to be close to an angry sibling? Anger becomes the volcano's way of life, and it works to the extent that it keeps others at a distance, thereby preventing possible pain. Perhaps volcanoes learn this behavior from observation, or even from being rejected or abused. Unfortunately, this response contributes significantly to sibling conflicts.

Remember the passage from Proverbs 22? Sadly, the last part of that verse—"lest you learn his ways"—so often comes true. Those who associate with volcanoes may end up becoming just like them.

In his autobiography, *Number 1,* former New York Yankees' manager Billy Martin tells about hunting with baseball star Mickey Mantle at Mickey's friend's ranch in Texas. When they reached the ranch, Mantle told Martin to wait in the car while he checked with his friend. Mantle's friend quickly gave them permission to hunt, but asked Mantle to do him a favor. He had a pet mule who was going blind, but he didn't have the heart to put the animal out of his misery. He asked Mantle to go out and shoot the mule for him.

When Mantle came back to the car, he pretended to be angry. He scowled, and slammed the door. Billy Martin asked him what was wrong. Mantle said his friend wouldn't let them hunt.

"I'm so mad at that guy," Mantle said, "I'm going out to his barn and shoot one of his mules!" Mantle drove like a maniac to the barn. Martin was shocked and he protested, but Mantle was adamant. "Just watch me!" he shouted.

When they got to the barn, Mantle jumped out of the car with his rifle, ran inside and shot the mule. As he was leaving, he heard two shots and ran back to the car. He saw that Martin had taken out his rifle, too.

"What are you doing?" Mantle yelled.

Martin, his face red with anger, yelled back, "We'll show that son of a gun! I just killed two of his cows!"

Remember, anger can be contagious. The only inoculation that counteracts it is the application of the Word of God. (For more information on this subject, see *When Anger Hits Home* by Gary Jackson Oliver and H. Norman Wright, Moody Press, 1992.)

TAKERS

Taking is another tactic that will drain a relationship. Most of us know how to give and take, but takers have perfected one way of relating. They love to receive and are experts at appearing helpless and dependent. Takers enjoy having others look after them. And usually it's more than just having someone else pick up the slack in their lives. Too often, takers are emotionally needy as well.

Siblings who are takers may call you again and again for advice, consolation and whatever else they can wangle out of you. Takers turn others into caretakers. They're like sponges, constantly soaking up everything you can give them. And don't expect anything in return! Taker siblings can be overbearing by their clinging and possessiveness of your time and energy. Some of them actually are in need at times, but taking seems to be their ongoing pattern for life. Some siblings control the entire clan by going from one to another with their needy dependency act, sucking out of each one whatever they can get. And if you don't offer to help or bail them out, how do you end up feeling? Guilty, of course!

It's as though takers live in constant crisis. When the other siblings get together, whom do they talk about? That's right; even then, the topic of conversation is controlled by the taker.

And that control continues until others stop being caregivers.
Les Parrott III has several practical suggestions for those
with taker siblings. First, make a list of your own needs, and
make sure you're meeting them. Doing this may alert you to the
tendency of having a compulsive need to help others. Then,
when the taker comes to you with a problem, ask him or her,
"What do you think you could do to solve the problem yourself?" or "If I weren't around, what would you do?" If the taker
responds with, "Gee, I don't know," then say, "Well, I don't know
either, but I'm sure you'll figure it out." At that point, turn and
walk away.[4]

Remember, no matter how much you do, how much you
give or how available you are, it will never be enough. You're
dealing with a bottomless pit. The best thing to do is learn to say
"No" or "I can't" or "I'm not available." If the taker asks why not,
just repeat what you said before, even if you sound like a broken
record (that is, if you're old enough to remember what a record
is!). Just repeat your original phrase again and again until they
quit asking. Don't give a reason. You're not obligated to give
one. If you do, you are only giving the taker more control. (See
When I Say No, I Feel Guilty by Manuel J. Smith, for assistance in
learning the broken-record technique.)

Learn to set boundaries. Don't do anything for a taker that
you are not prepared to do the rest of your life—because that is
exactly what he or she will come to expect. A helpful phrase in
setting boundaries is, "This is what I can do for you, but no
more."[5]

In so many of those tactics we've examined, the motive is the
same: control. Some siblings are blatant about using this device.
Others boast about it, which makes it worse.

My wife, Joyce, and I enjoy fishing. Over the years we've
collected a vast array of hooks, including single barb, double

barb, triple barb and barbless. Controllers are people who have learned to use hooks well—emotional hooks that definitely are not barbless! And once they get those hooks into you, it is no easy trick to dislodge them.

CONTROLLERS

Siblings use control to protect themselves from real or imagined concerns. It is part of their survival system, both in and out of the family. They see control as their best defense. They live in fear of the disastrous results and consequences of not being in control. They fear rejection, abandonment, hurt, disappointment and losing control itself. They also may be addicted to the respect, power or emotional rush they get from controlling others.

I've counseled numerous controllers. Their need to be in control is an integral part of their personalities. Some even have said, "I know I control. But why not? I have a lot to offer, and I know what I'm talking about. Why waste time? I want to see things happen—fast and efficiently. And I can do that!" What a sad attitude.

Controllers use a variety of methods to get you to do what they want. One ploy is indebtedness. Their message is, "You owe me," and this pushes your guilt button. Does this barbed statement—or some variation of it—sound familiar? "If it weren't for the good words I put in for you with my friend, you never would have had that opportunity, even if you are my brother."

Sarcasm is a favorite response of controllers. Most of us have felt its bite. Often the sarcastic tone and even nonverbal messages (which make up over 90 percent of the message in face-to-face conversation) are the means intended to control you. Consider a statement like, "Oh, sure, you remembered Mom's birthday. Then how come you planned to take off this weekend?" Not only are you dragged in by this emotional hook, but you can feel the irritation beginning to build. Your stomach churns. Your pulse quickens. The more you try to explain or defend yourself, the worse it gets. The accuser's sarcasm and disbelief just increase. In effect, the accuser is calling you a liar—and no one deals well with that sort of accusation.

One of the painful hooks controllers use is an assumed agreement with an underlying threat of criticism. "Karen, now stop and think about this for a minute. Then you'll see that I'm right, and it's best to go along with this. I always had to show you what to do when we were kids [the assumed agreement], and I still have to! Any intelligent adult could see this right away [underlying criticism]." Take the bait on this one, and you'll end up being reeled in.

Another hook makes you the victim of a forced choice. "Jim, tell me which day you can help me clean Mom's attic. I'd like to know now. Not tomorrow, but right now." The pressure begins to build. You'd better respond right away, whether you're ready to or not. Later, you'll probably feel anger not only toward your sibling but also at yourself for getting pulled into the trap.

In another clever method, the controller makes judgment statements, pretending to be the object of the judgment while making it clear that the statement is directed toward you. He or she says something like, "I should have known better. Letting you borrow that equipment was a mistake. It's my fault for letting you use it, and now it's ruined." Or how about this: "You really shouldn't let Dad run your life like that, you know. At 38, you need to be your own person. When are you going to break loose from his control?" Judgment statements inform you that the controller knows what's best for your life, more so than you do.

Every now and then I read or hear a disclaimer made by an organization or television station that goes something like this: "The views expressed by this speaker are not necessarily the views of the management of this station." I've heard controllers voice similar disclaimers: "I don't mean to be critical, but. . . ." or "I don't mean to be telling you how to run your life, but. . . ." The problem is, they really do want to run your life! They know it, and you know it. But you don't know what to do about it.

Sometimes a controller's criticism is hidden so deeply in a statement that it's difficult to confront directly. Embedded or implied criticism is like that. Often it's expressed in the form of a question, the hook being the delivery. In a somewhat incredulous tone of voice you hear, "You aren't actually going to come to Thanksgiving dinner after working out all morning, are you?" The message is that the controller doesn't approve of your plans, and you should know better.

Controllers use words that are absolutes, such as *always* and *never*. They also fail to give others the benefit of the doubt. You may have heard phrases like, "If it weren't for you. . . ." or "Because of you, I. . . ." These are blame and shame statements, which older siblings often learn to perfect at home. Responsibility for whatever has gone wrong in the controller's life is thrust onto your shoulders, whether valid or not. And the more defensive you become, the greater their level of deafness.

Controllers are clever. They often use blame shifting to get their point across. This way they don't have to shoulder any of the responsibility. "It doesn't bother me that you're not going to attend, but I think it's going to bother Mom and Dad. You know how they are!" Controllers can't seem to come out and be straight and truthful. If you try to confront them by asking if they too are bothered by your not attending, they will deny it.

I don't know anyone who enjoys a controlling sibling. There are times you may feel like pruning them from your family tree! Even though that's not possible, there are steps you can take to ensure your survival.

Steps for Survival

DON'T TAKE IT PERSONALLY

Stop taking what they say or do personally. It's true that siblings put pressure on you either to live up to their standards or to risk rejection from them. This is their lifestyle and habit pattern. As one author put it,

> Reframe your perception of them so that they seem less like villains or slave drivers or thorns in your side and more like relatively harmless robots with their wires crossed. Instead of getting knocked off your feet by the emotional undertow of an angry tirade, think of those shouting, foot-stomping, name-calling controllers as if they were children throwing tantrums to vent the frustration they do not know how to deal with in any other way.[6]

Don't look at your sibling as bad or wrong. Being judgmental only activates your anger. Think of their behavior as being a different way of seeing and doing things. In a way, this is applying 1 Corinthians 13:7 to the situation: "Love . . . is ever ready to believe the best of every person" (*AMP.*).

Remember, as controllers were growing up, they learned this was how to survive in life. Unfortunately, that lesson may have been learned at your expense.

Above all, don't accept the controller's perception or portrayal of you. Controllers try to change others because of their own need for control. If you discover an area of your life that does need change and correction, then take steps to do it for your own growth, not to please a controller.

CONTROL YOUR THOUGHTS

Bring your thoughts about your sibling under control. You're probably making the situation worse than it is by what is taking place in your thought life. When people are under the tyranny of a controller, they tend to think in ways that magnify the problem. Most of us tend to worry about what will happen if we don't live up to the expectations of others. We end up taking on some of the controller's thinking patterns and then live in fear of being criticized, rejected or ignored. Controllers constantly are on the lookout for whatever can go wrong. They tend to jump to conclusions, minimizing their own abilities and skills. They also tend to project past experiences with others into the future.

> *Most of us tend to worry about what will happen if we don't live up to the expectations of others. We end up taking on some of the controller's thinking patterns and then live in fear of being criticized, rejected or ignored.*

When you are caught in this sort of a situation with a controller, it's time to go back to God's Word for clarity, insight, guidance and strength. Let the Scriptures assist you in stabilizing your thoughts. Look at these passages and what they say about worry:

Anxiety in a man's heart weighs it down, but an encouraging word makes it glad (Prov. 12:25, *AMP.*).

All the days of the desponding and afflicted are made evil [by anxious thoughts and forebodings], but he who has a glad heart has a continual feast [regardless of circumstances] (15:15, *AMP*.).

Do not fret or have any anxiety about anything, but in every circumstance and in everything, by prayer and petition (definite requests), with thanksgiving, continue to make your wants known to God.

And God's peace [shall be yours, that tranquil state of a soul assured of its salvation through Christ, and so fearing nothing from God and being content with its earthly lot of whatever sort that is, that peace] which transcends all understanding shall garrison and mount guard over your hearts and minds in Christ Jesus.

For the rest, brethren, whatever is true, whatever is worthy of reverence and is honorable and seemly, whatever is just, whatever is pure, whatever is lovely and lovable, whatever is kind and winsome and gracious, if there is any virtue and excellence, if there is anything worthy of praise, think on and weigh and take account of these things [fix your minds on them].

Practice what you have learned and received and heard and seen in me, and model your way of living on it, and the God of peace (of untroubled, undisturbed well-being) will be with you (Phil. 4:6-9, *AMP*.).

With practice, you can learn to turn your thoughts off and on. That may help, but to do so you must put things in their proper perspective. The more you practice control, the greater the possibility of immediate control. We don't have to act in accordance with our feelings or negative thoughts.

Every time you have any kind of negative thought about your sibling or yourself, challenge it. Give yourself the benefit of the doubt. When you think about the problem, see yourself as being capable of handling it, rather than as a victim and your brother or sister as a villain. Don't continue to empower that sibling by your thinking.

FIND HEALTHY RELEASES

Find a healthy way to vent emotionally. You need to use methods that are different from those your controlling sibling uses. Burying your feelings is unhealthy for you emotionally, physically and spiritually. And dumping on yourself because of how you feel is no solution either. You need a safe, healthy outlet for what's building up inside. Express your feelings aloud in prayer—with no editing. You also can express them to a trusted friend of the same sex, a person who can listen and reflect back what you're feeling. Express those feelings through writing unmailed letters to your sibling, or keep a confidential journal.[7]

SET LIMITS

Evaluate what you will and won't tolerate. As you learn to release your feelings, you will discover that what your sibling does or says will no longer affect you as much. You may or may not be able to assist your sibling in modifying some aspects of his or her controlling behavior. But your new beliefs and responses will ease some of the pressure you once felt.

KEEP ADVICE TO YOURSELF

Don't bother telling your sibling that he or she should be less controlling. This is an exercise in futility, because a controller does not respond to the advice of others, however well-meaning. In fact, the typical controller will respond to this sort of approach by increasing the already controlling behavior patterns.

LEARN TO SHARE

Learn how to share your thoughts and feelings with your sibling. This is a necessary survival technique. Without it, you may lose your identity in this relationship. An example of this is: "When you remind me to call Mom and Dad, I really feel bothered. I will be calling them on my own time schedule, and then I'll call and let you know what they said."

Notice what's said in the above example: You share your feeling, identify the unacceptable behavior, follow with a request and then share what they will gain by responding to what you've said.

ESTABLISH BOUNDARIES

The violation of a person's boundaries can occur in many relationships, but it is especially prevalent in a relationship with a controller. Controllers become invasive and try to run your life for you. Thus, you need to determine what and how much you are willing to do with their demands. If more than one sibling is a controller, deal with each one separately.

Being an Encourager

Have you heard the term "damage control"? It's what a group or a person does to keep damage to a minimum. Children do this in a family. To counter what a sibling does, you develop your own strategy. It's like playing an ongoing game of checkers. Your sibling makes a move, and then you make one to protect your checkers. The game of checkers can go on for hours, but sibling games can go on for years.

It's all a process of maneuvering. When you're young, the moves are basic and simplistic. As you get older, you refine the moves, and they become a bit more difficult to identify. You used your responses and strategies as a child to defend yourself. So did your sibling. How long will you continue to use them? If someone doesn't decide to change things, these same responses and strategies could go on until you reach the other end of the life cycle. There's nothing stranger than to see senior citizen siblings reacting to each other as they did when they were children.

> *There's nothing stranger than to see senior*
> *citizen siblings reacting to each other*
> *as they did when they were children.*

There's a better way to respond to your siblings, regardless of their lifestyle, what they've done or how they feel about you. And it's not so much a defensive approach as an offensive one. It will probably seem quite unfamiliar, since it may go against the way you were reared. But it's a way of response that is a practical means of reflecting Christ's love as well as being an encourager to your siblings.

To be an encourager, you need to have an attitude of optimism. The *American Heritage Dictionary* has one of the better definitions of the word: a "tendency or disposition to expect the best possible outcome, or to dwell on the most hopeful aspect of a situation." When this is your attitude or perspective, you'll be able to encourage others. "Encouragement" means "to inspire; to continue on a chosen course; to impart courage or confidence."

Look at what God's Word tells us to do in relation to encouragement. In Acts 18:27, the word "encouraged" means "urged forward, persuaded." In 1 Thessalonians 5:11, "encourage" means "to stimulate another person to the ordinary duties of life." You may have a sibling who needs just such encouragement. Consider the words found in the *Amplified* version of 1 Thessalonians 5:14:

> And we earnestly beseech you, brethren, admonish (warn and seriously advise) those who are out of line [the loafers, the disorderly, and the unruly]; encourage the timid and fainthearted, help and give your support to the weak souls, [and] be very patient with everybody [always keeping your temper].

Maybe you have some siblings in your life who fit the above description.

The Greek word in that verse from 1 Thessalonians, translated "encourage" (*paramutheomai*), means "to console, comfort, and cheer up." This process includes elements of understanding, redirecting of thoughts and a general shifting of focus from the negative to the positive. In the context of the verse, it refers to the timid or fainthearted individual who is discouraged and ready to give up. Encouraging a person in this manner is a matter of lending your faith and hope to the person until his or her own faith develops. Do you have any siblings who need this sort of encouragement?

The word "help" (*anechomai*) primarily contains the idea of "taking interest in, being devoted to, rendering assistance, or holding up spiritually and emotionally." It is not so much an active involvement as a passive approach. It suggests the idea of coming alongside a person and acting as a support. In the context of 1 Thessalonians 5:14, it seems to refer to those who are incapable of helping themselves. Can you think of a time when this kind of help was needed by any of your siblings?

First Thessalonians 5:11 states, "Therefore encourage one

another and build each other up, just as in fact you are doing."
Hebrews 3:13 says we're to "encourage one another daily." In the
setting of this verse, encouragement is associated with protecting the believer from callousness. Hebrews 10:25 says, "Let us
encourage one another." This time the word means to keep
those on their feet who, if left to themselves, would collapse.
Your encouragement serves as the concrete pilings in a structural
support.

The Word of God is very clear about how we're to handle
these sorts of situations. To be a consistent encourager, you will
need to reflect the character qualities of 1 Corinthians 13. Here
they are, amplified in a unique way:

- Patient (tolerant of frailties, imperfections and short-
  comings of your siblings)
- Kind (tender, thoughtful toward your siblings)
- Not jealous (of their accomplishments, abilities or even
  favored position)
- Not boastful (about your personal appearance or achieve-
  ments in an attempt to compete with your siblings)
- Not arrogant (not disdainful of your sibling's achieve-
  ments)
- Not rude (not inconsiderate of their needs or beliefs)
- Not insistent on your own way (willing to compromise)
- Not irritable (especially at family get-togethers)
- Not resentful (not holding grudges; forgiving)
- Not rejoicing in wrong (not delighting in your sibling's
  misfortunes; not keeping score of perceived wrongs)
- Rejoicing in right (encouraging others for who they
  are, and also when they get the limelight)
- Bearing all things (supporting your siblings in times of
  struggle by offers of assistance and prayer)

• Hoping all things (not wallowing in pessimism about your relationship; keeping a positive attitude)
• Enduring all things (believing that your relationship can improve).[8]

At the end of that chapter, the apostle Paul says that we are to put away childish things (see v. 11). There's a better way to live, and it's found in not being defensive but in being honest, forthright and free from the responses that push your buttons. You don't have to keep playing the sibling game. You can choose responses that are different and healthy, and that reflect your relationship with the Lord Jesus Christ.

Notes
1. Drs. William and Madra Hapworth and Joan Rathner Heilman, *Mom Loved You Best* (New York: Viking Penguin, 1993), p. 134, adapted.
2. Les Parrott III, *High Maintenance Relationships* (Wheaton, Ill.: Tyndale House, 1996), pp. 23-33, adapted.
3. Ibid., pp. 122-28, adapted.
4. Ibid., pp. 141-46, adapted.
5. Ibid.
6. Miriam Elliott and Susan Meltsner, *The Perfectionist Predicament* (New York: William Morrow and Co., 1991), pp. 262-63, adapted.
7. Steven Hendlin, *When Good Is Never Enough* (New York: G.P. Putnam's Sons, 1992), pp. 205-10, adapted.
8. Dr. Richard Matteson and Janis Long Harris, *What If I Married the Wrong Person?* (Minneapolis, Minn.: Bethany House Publishers, 1996), pp. 116-17, adapted.

Chapter Nine

The Games Siblings Play

"Bang! I got you. You're dead!"

Cops and robbers, cowboys and Indians or paper dolls—the games you played with your brothers and sisters probably were varied. Play took up much of your time as a child. Some games were active, some quiet. Some were intense, others mellow. Perhaps one sibling always had to win, while another just enjoyed the game. One even may have expected to end up the loser most of the time. One played by the rules, another didn't.

Games can be just that—games. But they also can reflect the patterns and interactions that occur in adult relationships. I imagine just about all children have played hide-and-seek or tag; some siblings continue to play these games as adults. I've seen some brothers and sisters who play hide-and-seek by pulling away from the family and isolating themselves. They may be available physically, but you still have to seek out and find where they are emotionally and relationally. Others, like ships in the Bermuda Triangle, disappear totally from family gatherings.

In the game of tag, someone is always "it." You may have a sibling who constantly tags you in some way, and you end up feeling like you're "it."

Most children also have played musical chairs. In this game, everyone walks around a group of chairs while the music plays. When the music stops, everyone rushes for a chair. The problem is that there is always one less chair than children looking for a seat. The unfortunate child who can't find a chair must leave the game. If that's ever happened to you, you know what it feels like to be "odd man out." Some adult siblings feel that way, especially at family gatherings. It may be that others get the attention, and you get the leftovers. Perhaps you've got some superachievers as siblings, and you never seem to measure up.

Variations of Games

One of the games adult siblings play is "never enough." You may graciously help one of your siblings who's struggling with serious problems. You go above and beyond the call of duty, and what kind of response do you get in return? Not much, if any. You end up feeling unappreciated for what you did, and even may be criticized for not doing more or for not doing exactly what was expected. You're left with the thoughts, *Why? Where did I go wrong—or did I? Is there something wrong with me, or is it them?*

Some siblings just aren't appreciative of what you do. They're overly focused on their own issues. They don't have concern for others' needs or efforts. And it's not unusual for you to get a negative response from your sibling in order to get you to continue to do more. Sometimes this expectation is placed upon the responsible one, who may be the oldest sibling.

You may find a variation of this type of sibling, one who wants your assistance or involvement; but when you make suggestions or extend offers to help, the door slams in your face. At that point, you feel set up, rejected, like a fish that rose to the bait but got tossed back for being undersized. Siblings who play this game really don't want help. They just want to dump their frustration on someone else. On the other hand, they can be very selective when they actually do want help; and if you're not right on target, your help won't be accepted. It's irritating when a genuine offer is made, and then the selection is picked over. But you need to remember that the defect is not in your offering, it's in that sibling's game playing and inability to receive graciously.

Just as much of a problem is the insatiable "starving" sibling. The word "enough" is not in their vocabulary. You give them an abundance of your time and attention, but it's barely a drop in the bucket. When you pull back to regroup, you're made to feel as though you haven't done anything at all. Not only is this sibling excessively needy, but he or she is quite adept at pushing your guilt button through statements, nonverbal messages, sighs and whatever means possible to keep the contributions coming.

Numerous families end up with a sibling who seems to know no other response than to react as a martyr. No matter what happens in martyrs' lives or how much others try to help or give them, they somehow find a way to turn every gift and every event into a tragedy or burden for themselves. "Nobody knows the trouble I've seen" is their theme song.

Have you experienced a threatening sibling? You know, the kind who uses threats, extortion or blackmail to get others to respond? Here's an example of the kind of blackmail a threatening sibling might use: "Mom always wondered what happened that summer, and unless you lend me the money I need, she'll hear about it. And that will break her heart. Is that what you want to happen?"

Identifying Emotions and
Setting Limits

Fortunately, not all siblings play these games. But if you do have siblings who respond in any of these negative ways, there are two steps you can take: First, identify the emotions that are evoked by their behavior; second, learn to avoid getting hooked into your siblings' negative game playing by setting limits on the relationships.

Whether we have difficulty in our relationships with parents, coworkers or siblings, emotions will be involved. We all have buttons that activate these emotions, and it doesn't take long for others to learn how to push them.

Perhaps you have a sibling guilt button. Others will use it to keep you stuck in responding to their games. Often guilt comes into play in the struggle between saying yes or no. Many find it easier to say yes to others and no to themselves, even when the commitment is not in their best interests. I've seen siblings who have struggled with a demanding, ungrateful sibling for years, unable to say no to their requests. This was extremely painful, but as soon as they tried to disengage from this sibling, guilt came rushing back. One man said, "I'm exhausted trying to deal with my sister. Every now and then I decide to take the time and energy I've been giving to her and give it back to myself. It feels great for a while. But I break down because of the guilt."

You may have a sibling who wants you to feel guilty. It's his or her way of hooking and controlling you. Jim's siblings knew exactly how to get through to him. He told about an incident that took place one Christmas:

> I'd had a great year at work, and had won a free trip to a
> ski resort in a neighboring state. Since Jean and I didn't

have kids yet but were planning to the next year, we decided this might be our last chance to take such a trip. The trip started two days before Christmas and ended three days after. About six weeks before, we let Mom know about it and she seemed all right with it. But then we got phone calls from my brother and sister. I heard statements like these:

- What do you mean, you're not coming for Christmas? We always get together.
- That's sure selfish of you to leave the family for what you want to do.
- You can't not be there. You hold things together for everyone. We wouldn't know what to do.
- You know Mom's getting up in years. This could be her last Christmas.
- You'll break Mom's heart. She won't say anything; but remember, you're the firstborn, and she relies on you.

On Christmas day they called to tell me everything that went wrong and how Mom missed me. We had a miserable time. The guilt wasn't worth it.

Harnessing Guilt

What do you do with the guilt you experience as a sibling? There are several steps you can take to harness this guilt. First, consider why guilt arises. Isn't it a response that occurs when we've done something wrong? Usually. So what is it that you've done in your current interaction with your sibling that's wrong? If you think it really is wrong, would it stand up in a court of law? Probably not. Who are the judge and jury in this situation? You or your siblings? Does the word "should" come into play here? All too often it does: "I should [or shouldn't] have . . ." will generate all sorts of guilt.

Perhaps the guilt feelings come into play because of expectations—yours, theirs or both. What are the expectations you have for yourself as they relate to your siblings? We all have them. Have you ever identified them and written them down? What about the expectations your siblings have for you? Have they clarified them and shared them with you? Probably not. It's like a silent game everyone plays. There's a hidden agenda, and the players are acting out a script, but it's not in writing.

Again, not all siblings do this. But for those who do, this step of sharing could help: In premarital counseling—and often with married couples—we ask them to make a list of 25 expectations they have for the other person. Once this is done, they exchange their lists, and each identifies which expectations are reasonable and can be met, and which ones are not and cannot be met. All of this is discussed, giving greater clarity to the relationship.

Your guilt may be activated when you change the way you respond to your sibling. The sibling doesn't like the change, so out come the weapons. What can you do? This may be a strange suggestion, but try learning to live with some guilt! Accept your feelings of guilt, and quit fighting them. You might say to yourself, *All right, I do feel guilty. I don't particularly want to, but I do, so I'll just accept it. I can live with that. It's not the end of the world. It won't incapacitate me. I'll give it permission to be a part of my life, and its presence doesn't mean I've done anything wrong or bad. It doesn't mean I have to change my mind on what I said to my sibling, either. What I did was all right, and I'll probably do it again. I can handle this.*

You want to come to the place where you accept how you have responded and can say, *What I did and said was healthy for both of us. I responded in a Christian way.* You want to learn to accept who you are in your relationship with your siblings. They may not find what you have said or done acceptable. They may not even find you acceptable at times. When this happens, tell yourself, *I can accept this. I can handle this. I'm not to live my life for their approval.* It could be that nothing you do will ever be acceptable to one of your siblings.[1] If this occurs and you start berating yourself, stop and remember the One to whom you are totally acceptable—God. Jesus Christ and His work on the Cross have made you totally acceptable to our heavenly Father.

Pleasing the One Who Matters Most

Don't put your worth and value in how your siblings see you or respond to you. Sure, we've all blown it, made mistakes and offended others. Perhaps you have the forgiveness of your siblings, perhaps not. It could be they'll always focus on what they perceive as your negative side. But you don't have to see it that way. You can view yourself as God does. When you remember that and rest in it, perhaps you can stop striving to win the approval of someone who may not have the capability of giving it.

Our understanding of who God is and how He wants to enrich our lives comes when we realize that He is committed to performing good in our lives. Consider God's Word:

> Surely goodness and love will follow me all the days of my life, and I will dwell in the house of the Lord forever (Ps. 23:6).

> I will make an everlasting covenant with them: I will never stop doing good to them . . . . I will rejoice in doing them good and will assuredly plant them in this land with all my heart and soul (Jer. 32:40,41).

A few years ago, the choir at our church sang an anthem based on Zephaniah 3:17. I had never heard the song before. The words were printed in our church bulletin, and I have read them many times since because they encourage, inspire and remind me of what I mean to God:

> And the Father will dance over you in joy!
> He will take delight in whom He loves.
> Is that a choir I hear singing the praises of God?
> No, the Lord God Himself is exulting over you in song!
> And He will joy over you in song!
> My soul will make its boast in God,
> For He has answered all my cries.
> His faithfulness to me is as sure as the dawn of a new
>   day.
> Awake my soul and sing!
> Let my spirit rejoice in God!
> Sing, O daughter of Zion, with all of your heart!
> Cast away fear for you have been restored!
> Put on the garment of praise as on a festival day.
> Join with the Father in glorious, jubilant song.
> God rejoices over you in song![2]

In his fascinating book *The Pleasures of God,* John Piper beautifully expresses how God desires to do good to all who hope in Him. Dr. Piper talks about God singing and asks, "What would it be like if God sang?"

> What do you hear when you imagine the voice of God singing?
>
> I hear the booming of Niagara Falls mingled with the trickle of a mossy mountain stream. I hear the blast of Mount Saint Helens mingled with a kitten's purr.

I hear the power of an East Coast hurricane and the barely audible puff of a night snow in the woods. And I hear the unimaginable roar of the sun, 865,000 miles thick, 1,300,000 times bigger than the earth, and nothing but fire, 1,000,000 degrees centigrade on the cooler surface of the corona. But I hear this unimaginable roar mingled with the tender, warm crackling of logs in the living room on a cozy winter's night.

I stand dumfounded, staggered, speechless that he is singing over me—one who has dishonored him so many times and in so many ways. It is almost too good to be true. He is rejoicing over my good with all his heart and all his soul. He virtually breaks forth into song when he hits upon a new way to do me good.[3]

Did you catch the significance of how God feels about you and what He wants for you? Do you get a sense of how important you are? What a confirmation that you are adequate!

A Balanced Response

Now, with that in mind, how can you respond to your sibling? Let's consider some common problems. One of your siblings wants to borrow money and has a track record of not paying back what he or she has borrowed. But your sibling claims to be desperate, says you're the only one who can help, and he or she needs that help right now. What do you do?

You can listen, explain that you need to think and pray about it for a day and that you'll respond tomorrow. If he or she persists, just use the same words and say the phrase again and again, no matter what. Don't allow yourself to be pressured or bullied. Then if you decide not to lend the money (which is probably what you'd decide in this situation), just explain that it wouldn't be a good idea and could lead to resentment on both sides. Tell your sibling that you do not believe it's in the best interests of the ongoing relationship. If he or she wishes, you'd be willing to help find other alternatives, but you will not be lending the money. Remember, it's all right if your sibling does not like your decision, or even like you, at this time.

Perhaps you have a sibling who makes too many unreasonable demands on your time. You could explain that you will set up some times that will be exclusively for the two of you. But you will have to stick to it unless there's an emergency. (Be sure you define ahead of time what an emergency is!)

If your sibling constantly picks at you and finds fault with you, you have some strategies available to you. First, to get a critic to back off, you can admit that you're not perfect, even mentioning your shortcomings before your sibling does. Second, when you're criticized, you can go along with what has been said, but do not defend yourself or give an excuse. Defenses or excuses are other names for fueling your sibling's fire! Let's look at some examples of proper responses on your part:

- Sibling: "Well, I see you're late again. I sure wish you could learn to be on time once in your life."
  You: "That's true. I am several minutes late."

- Sibling: "You ought to eat better. You're always stuffing your mouth with that junk food."
  You: "You could be right about that."

- Sibling: "I wish you would have dressed up better for this event. You've dressed in your old usual way."
  You: "That's right. I am dressed in my usual way."

- Sibling: "I don't know when you're going to grow up. You act the same way you did as a kid."
  You: "Well, that's a possibility."

- Sibling: "You're such a tightwad. You won't help anyone out even if they're desperate. You keep it just for yourself!"
  You: "That's probably true."

Fighting a Fogbank Is Futile

Do you see how you can respond? You are not denying the attack or criticism. You are not defensive, nor do you attack your sibling. You're responding in a way that often is referred to as "fogging." I'm sure you've been in a fogbank before. A fogbank is persistent and just hangs in there. You never know when it will lift. You can't see through it clearly, and when you try to penetrate it, there's no resistance. It doesn't fight back. If you throw a rock at it, there's no hard surface, so it can't ricochet back. It goes right through it. In time, anyone with any sense will give up trying to do anything about the fog and just leave it alone.

So when you're criticized, you can handle it by offering no resistance to strike against. That doesn't mean you agree exactly with what has been said. You've agreed with the part that's true, with the principle of what's been said or with the odds of the statement. And if you're thinking this will never work with your sibling, how do you know unless you think about it, practice it and then do it? You have nothing to lose, especially if what you're doing now isn't working.[4]

This approach also is in keeping with the biblical pattern of responding:

Don't refuse to accept criticism; get all the help you can (Prov. 23:12, *TLB*).

It is a badge of honor to accept valid criticism (25:12, *TLB*).

A man who refuses to admit his mistakes can never be successful. But if he confesses and forsakes them, he gets another chance (28:13, *TLB*).

Repay no one evil for evil, but take thought for what is honest and proper and noble [aiming to be above reproach] in the sight of everyone. Do not let yourself be overcome by evil, but overcome (master) evil with good (Rom. 12:17,21, *AMP.*).

Then let us no more criticize and blame and pass judgment on one another, but rather decide and endeavor never to put a stumbling block or an obstacle or a hindrance in the way of a brother. So let us then definitely aim for and eagerly pursue what makes for harmony and for mutual upbuilding (edification and development) of one another (14:13,19, *AMP.*).

The Sibling Anger Button

Perhaps you have a "sibling anger button." This may not be the response you want to give, but it's so easy to allow that spark of irritation to begin to grow into an intense flame. Your anger may come out as a heat-seeking missile or something more subtle. In the previous chapter, we talked about your sibling's anger. Now let's consider yours.

If you get angry at a sibling on a consistent basis, do you understand why? One woman said, "Oh, I know why. He wants me to get angry. He just delights in getting me upset. He'd tease me as a child until I flipped out, and now he's doing it as an adult. I just hate him when he goads me into getting angry. And I hate myself for falling into that trap and getting angry. What can I do? Help me!"

> *The three main causes of anger are fear, hurt and frustration. Anger toward a sibling is a secondary emotion.*

There are times when we need to be angry at things that are wrong or unjust. But anger in sibling relationships usually isn't for that reason. It's often one of the childhood games that we drag along with us into adult life. Too often it's destructive. It erects barriers. It doesn't draw people close but puts distance between them. You might have a sibling who is described in the following verse; if so, you'll need wisdom in learning to deal with him or her:

Do not make friends with a hot-tempered man, do not associate with one easily angered, or you may learn his ways and get yourself ensnared (Prov. 22:24,25).

Keep in mind that your anger toward your sibling is a secondary emotion, a clue or a warning sign that you're experiencing something else. The three main causes of anger are fear, hurt and frustration. Some may be afraid of a particular sibling, and that's what prompts the anger. Many are hurt by what a sibling does or says, and that's what prompts their anger. Most are frustrated by what a sibling does or says, and that really pushes their buttons.

When others don't act the way we want, when they ignore us, attack us and refuse to change, frustration is a typical response. And it's the first step of anger. But remember, anger does not have to be unleashed in a manner that will hurt or destroy. Instead, it can be used in a constructive manner to eliminate frustration.

Reacting with anger to a sibling is like pouring gasoline on a fire that is already blazing. A chemical retardant would be far more effective. Proverbs 15:1 illustrates an appropriate response: "A soft answer turns away wrath, but a harsh word stirs up anger" (*NKJV*).

I hear people in my office and in my seminars say to me again and again, "Norm, I don't want to talk in an angry way to others, especially to my brothers and sisters, but something just comes over me and I let it rip! There's a limit to what I can take. I know I really love them, but sometimes I don't like them very much. I don't know what to do to change."

I usually respond with a question: "When you feel frustrated and angry with your siblings, what do you focus on: how they react to what you said or how you would like them to act?"

They usually reply, "Oh, I keep mulling over what I didn't like and my destructive comments. I relive it again and again and beat up on myself for hurting them."

I then ask, "Do you realize that by rehearsing your failures you are programming yourself to repeat them?" They usually respond with a puzzled look. But it's true. When you spend so much time thinking about what you *shouldn't* have done, you simply reinforce that behavior. Furthermore, spending all your time and energy mentally rehashing your failures keeps you from formulating what you really want to do. Redirecting your time and energy toward a solution will make a big difference in how you want to respond to your frustration. And then you'll find that you really will experience change!

Reducing Frustration

Let's consider several steps you can take to reduce your frustration and curb the words you don't want to express.

The first step is to find someone with whom you can share your concerns and develop an accountability relationship. Select someone who will be willing to pray with you and check on you regularly to see how you're doing.

You also need to be honest and accountable to yourself and others about changes you want to make. Take a sheet of paper and respond in writing to the following questions:

- How do you feel about becoming frustrated? Be specific. How do you feel about getting angry? There are some people who enjoy their frustration and anger. It gives them an adrenaline rush and a feeling of power. Does this description fit you in any way?
- When you are frustrated, do you want to be in control of your response, or do you want to be spontaneous? In other words, do you want to decide what to do or just let your feelings take you where they want to go?
- If you want to stay in control, how much time and energy are you willing to spend to make this happen? For change to occur, the motivational level needs to remain both constant and high.
- When you are bothered by something that someone else does, how would you like to respond? What would you like to say at that time? Be specific.

There is a reason why God inspired men to write the Scriptures and why He preserved His words through the centuries for us: God's guidelines for life are the best! Regardless of what you may have experienced or have been taught in the past, God's plan works.

Write out each of the following verses from Proverbs on separate index cards:

> Reckless words pierce like a sword, but the tongue of the wise brings healing (12:18).

> A patient man has great understanding, but a quick-tempered man displays folly (14:29).

> Better a patient man than a warrior, a man who controls his temper than one who takes a city (16:32).

Add to your card file other scriptures you discover that relate to frustration and anger. Read these verses aloud morning and evening for three weeks, and you will own them.

Your intentions may be good, but once the frustration/anger sequence kicks into gear, your ability to think clearly is limited. You will be able to change only if you plan to change. Remember, your sibling may not change, but you can.

Identify in advance what you want to say when you begin to feel frustrated. Be specific. Write out your responses and read them aloud to yourself. In my counseling office, I often have clients practice their new responses on me, and I attempt to respond as the other person would. By practicing on me, they are able to refine their statements, eliminate their anxiety or feelings of discomfort and gain confidence for their new approach. Your spouse or prayer partner could assist you this way.

Be Slow to Anger

Begin training yourself to delay your verbal and behavioral responses when you recognize that you're frustrated. The book of Proverbs repeatedly admonishes us to be slow to anger. You must slow down your responses if you want to change any verbal habits you have cultivated over the years. When we allow frustration and anger to be expressed unhindered, these emotions are like a runaway locomotive. You need to catch them before they gather momentum, so you can switch the tracks and steer them in the right direction.[5]

One helpful way to change direction is to use a trigger word. Whenever you feel frustration and anger rising within you, remind yourself to slow down and gain control by saying something to yourself like "stop," "think," "control" and so on. These are trigger words that will help you switch gears and put your new plan into action.

One of the approaches I often suggest to defuse a frustrating situation is this: Mentally give your sibling permission to be involved in the behavior that frustrates you. This approach gives you time to implement a levelheaded plan.

I'm not suggesting that you emotionally give up and allow others to do anything they want. There are some behaviors that are highly detrimental and require a direct response. But I am suggesting that there are steps you can take to keep yourself from being sucked into other people's negative behavior patterns and to break some of those patterns within yourself.

Soothing Self-Talk

Your inner conversation—also called "self-talk"—is where your frustrations are either tamed or inflamed. What you say to others and how you behave is determined by how you talk to yourself about their behaviors and responses. Self-talk is the words and ideas you think to yourself. In fact, your most powerful emotions—anger, depression, guilt and worry—are initiated and fed by your inner conversations. Changing your inner conversa-tion is essential to keep your frustrations from erupting into wounding words with your sibling.

> *Your most powerful emotions—anger, depression, guilt and worry—are initiated and fed by your inner conversations.*

There will be times when you know in advance that you're in a situation that may lead to someone getting angry—especially when that someone is you. If you pay attention to your self-talk—the words you usually say to yourself in this sort of situa-tion—you will be able to identify two things: what it is that gen-erates your anger and what you can do to adjust your attitude. You also will discover your expectations so that the situation can be less anger-producing. Here are some samples of anger-reduc-ing self-talk:

- I won't take what is said or done personally.
- No matter what happens, I know I can learn to control my frustrations and anger. I have this capability because of the presence of Jesus in my life and because of His strength, which He gives to me.
- I am going to stay calm and in control.
- I will respond to statements that usually trigger me, with statements like this: "That's interesting"; "I'll think about that"; "Could you tell me more about this situation?"
- I don't have to allow this situation to bother me.

- If I begin to get upset, I will take some deep breaths, slow down, delay my responses and purposely speak more softly.[6]

One of the best ways to reduce your frustration is to accept the fact that your sibling may never become the person you want him or her to be. This can take some pressure off of you. Remember also, you can't live your siblings' lives for them.

There is a possibility that, once you begin to respond in a new way, your sibling may intensify his or her attempts to make you angry. When you change, you create a big hole in the system. The balance is off, and others will work twice as hard to bring it back to its original position.

Other Sibling Buttons

There are other sibling buttons besides anger and frustration, and some siblings are adept at pushing them. Have you ever been embarrassed by what a sibling does or the difficulties he or she gets into? An older man once told me, "I've been embarrassed by my brother most of my life. I don't even like to be in social situations with him. He's been out of work more than he's been in, and I hate when others ask me how he's doing. Sometimes, if it were possible, I'd like to divorce him!"

Perhaps the most problematic response toward your siblings is ambivalence. You're numb because of all the conflicting emotions. You love your older sister, but you also hate her. You feel compassion as well as contempt. You want to help, but you are also repelled by her. Because of these polarized emotions, you've checked out in some way or form. You may want to resolve the issues, and you may not. It's difficult to find a resolution for ambivalence.

Set Limits and Boundaries

What else can you do with siblings who seem to invade your life emotionally? The simple answer is to set limits. When you set limits, you set up boundaries. Without boundaries and limits, you could end up with a sibling who invades your domain like Iraq invaded Kuwait—and with almost as much destruction.

Remember this about setting limits: It's not rejection, even though this is the predominant feeling you and/or your siblings may experience when limits are set. Setting limits means taking care of yourself, doing what's best for your sibling and ending your caretaking. You are shifting the responsibility for your sibling's life back to where it belongs—from your shoulders to his or hers. Setting limits prevents you from overinvolvement but not from caring for your brother or sister. Setting limits is acting upon the realization that you can't solve someone else's problems or live someone else's life.

IDENTIFY THE EMOTIONS

So, how do you set limits between yourself and your siblings? First, identify the feeling that you usually experience in your interactions with them. Is it guilt? What about anger, fear or embarrassment? Or are you numb? Do you feel controlled, manipulated, put upon? If these feelings are continual, they're sending you a clear and concise message—you need to set limits!

Setting limits takes careful thought and wisdom. Where should the limits be set? Some go overboard and almost cut off siblings entirely. This is not what I'm suggesting (even though at times you may have wanted to do just that). Some people don't go far enough. They end up setting token limits, which really aren't limits at all. How much is too much and how much is not enough? There are no set answers; only you can decide that for yourself.

JUST SAY NO

The two important words—"set limits"—have a companion word—"no!" Setting limits means refusing in some instances, and responding in new and different ways. A simple but firm no is sometimes all that is necessary. But don't add too much information to your no. Keep it clear and firm. Be specific, so your sibling knows what to expect. You may struggle with this approach, as Ken did:

> I felt so bad. My brother lost his job and wanted me to do two things: put in a good word for him where I work, so he could get a job, and then lend him money. I couldn't or wouldn't do either. He's my brother, but he wouldn't last at a job at my work. I would be lying, and hurting my company, if I gave him a recommendation. A loan? That's a joke. It would be gone forever. He never pays back money. I hate to see him broke and out on the street, but I have to survive, myself. I can't fix him. He has to want to be fixed.

OTHER ALTERNATIVES

There are other ways to set limits. Are you too available? Do you jump when your siblings beckon? If so, why? You're teaching them to expect you to be available. Set limits on your time—both when and how much.

You may involve your siblings in setting limits by asking them to come up with some alternatives and compromises to their request. This will require some give-and-take on both sides.

Rescuing

When I was in high school and college, some of my friends had summer jobs as lifeguards on the beaches and at public pools.

To me, lifeguarding was a dream job. These guys were in the sun all day, usually surrounded by kids their own age. The hours were good and the scenery was great! As summer came to an end, I'd say to them, "What a great summer job you had! I'll bet you're sorry it's over."

Many of them surprised me by saying, "Not really. I'm glad to be getting back to school. I'm tired of constantly rescuing people."

When it comes to relationships, some people never tire of being rescuers. In fact, they live for it. But there's a problem with that. A relationship is not going to work if either one habitually rescues the other—even when that other one is a sibling.

Sometimes you may be the one who takes the initiative to rescue. Or perhaps it is your siblings who insist that you help, either by solving their problems or protecting them from the consequences of their own behavior. Neither of these approaches leads to a healthy relationship.

When you rescue on a continual basis, you're teaching others that there's no need to change, because you'll be there to bail them out. They won't learn from past blunders either. Also, if you rescue them so regularly that others are aware of it, their reinforcing comments will tend to keep you locked into that pattern of behavior.

When you rescue others, what do you expect in return? Thanks, appreciation, perhaps even reciprocation? With siblings, you often will find this response lacking—especially if your sibling is a habitual taker. This is because when you rescue others, you are exerting some type of control over them; in time, they can end up resenting you for it. The unspoken, subtle message conveyed to them is, "I'm better than you are, and you're not capable of handling this yourself."[7]

"Drainage" Issues

The two major "drainage" issues with siblings are time and money. Some drain you of advice, while others drain you of money. It's always risky to lend money to anyone, particularly a sibling who is known to be a taker. You're not a bank or a loan company. Perhaps you need to ask yourself these questions if you're thinking of lending money:

- Can I afford to think of this money as a gift rather than a loan, since I may never get it back?
- Is this money that rightfully belongs more to my family than to my sibling?
- If the money isn't paid back, can I move on in my life without resentment?

If you lend money to a sibling, you may want to think of it as a gift and hope to see it repaid. If you're blessed with money and wouldn't miss it, losing this amount won't jeopardize you financially. If your sibling is trustworthy and dependable, lending him or her money won't hurt or hinder your relationship. If the sibling agrees to a consistent payment plan, in writing, then there's a possibility that it may work out.

Remember, when you set limits—whether in regard to the two drainage issues of time and money or to anything else— you're the only one who has to like those limits and agree to them. Don't look to your sibling to validate what you're doing.[8] This is your decision, and it needs to be made for your benefit as well as for your sibling's. The result will be a healthier, more loving adult relationship.

Notes

1. Dr. Jane Greer with Edward Myers, *Adult Sibling Rivalry* (New York: Crown Publishing, 1992), pp. 62-70, adapted.

2. "And the Father Will Dance." Lyrics adapted from Zephaniah 3:14,17 and Psalm 54:2,4, arranged by Mark Hayes.

3. John Piper, *The Pleasures of God* (Portland, Ore.: Multnomah Press, 1991), p. 188.

4. Manuel J. Smith, Ph.D., *When I Say No I Feel Guilty* (New York: Bantam Books, 1975), pp. 104-9, adapted.

5. H. Norman Wright, *Winning Over Your Emotions* (Eugene, Ore.: Harvest House, 1998), pp. 67-71, adapted.

6. Gary Hawkins with Carol Hawkins, *Prescription for Anger* (New York: Warner Books, 1988), pp. 196-98, adapted.

7. H. Norman Wright, *Relationships That Work (and Those That Don't)* (Ventura, Calif.: Regal Books, 1998), pp. 115, 116, adapted.

8. Greer and Myers, *Adult,* pp. 90-100, adapted.

Chapter Ten

The Loss of a Sibling

If one of your brothers or sisters has died, you're a "forgotten griever." There are other names for you as well, such as the "lonely mourner." There is no other loss in either childhood or adulthood that seems to be so neglected as the death of a brother or a sister.

When a sibling dies, very few take into account the depth of a bond that can occur between two siblings. Often it seems that others make light of such a loss. If you've lost an adult sibling, you may have heard insensitive responses as, "Just be glad it wasn't your child or your spouse." It's as though the death of a sibling is dismissed, since a brother or sister is not considered one of the central characters of your life. So in addition to losing your sibling, you lose the support of others during your grief. Indeed, you do feel like a lonely mourner.[1]

Many begin this struggle with a loss in childhood. A century ago there wasn't as much reaction to the death of a child as there is today, because the child mortality rate was much higher then.

At the end of the last century, as many as 200 out of 1,000 infants under the age of one year died from various diseases. Families tended to have several children so that some would survive. As childhood mortality has declined, the thought of a child dying seems remote. Therefore, when it does occur, there is a greater impact than ever before.

The Effects on Parents

The death of a child is unlike any other loss. It's a horrendous shock, no matter how it happens. It's important to comprehend the impact this has on parents in order to understand why they respond to the remaining children in the way they do.

One of the most difficult and disturbing issues to handle is the "wrongness" of a child's death. It just shouldn't happen. It doesn't make sense. It's death out of turn. The parent often feels, *Why should I survive when our child, who should have survived, didn't?* Death violates the cycle of the young growing up and replacing the old.

Grief over the loss of a child is disabling. Even for someone who has experienced other losses, there is no precedent for losing a child. Nothing prepares a parent for such a tragedy. The loss of a child casts a shadow on the parent's life. Recently I read a statement that expressed grief as a shadow on the moon that darkens the night into almost unbearable darkness. The shadow must pass slowly across the moon's face before the light is restored. But with a child's death, the shadow moves at a snail's pace and sometimes becomes stuck.[2]

When parents lose a child, they also lose what that child represented to them. They feel victimized in so many ways. They feel as though they've lost part of themselves, even part of their physical body. Those features in the child that bore resemblance to either parent seem to magnify the loss.

Parents miss the physical interaction as well—the sight, sound, smell and touch of their child. If they were still in the hands-on, caregiving stage with their child, this absence will be terribly painful.

The child embodied their connection to the future, too, and that no longer exists. If the child was old enough to respond to them, they've lost a very special love source. That love was based on need, dependence, admiration and appreciation, but now it's gone. They've lost some of their own treasured qualities and talents as well, for they saw some of those that they valued most in their child. Further, they've lost the expectations and dreams they had for their child as he or she grew older. The anticipated years, full of so many special events, were ripped away.

Parents also may see their child's death as a failure on their part. They may feel anger and frustration over their inability to exert some control over what happened to their child.[3]

With the death of their child a parent feels he or she has failed in the basic function of parenthood: taking care of the children and the family. A parent is supposed to protect and provide for their child. They are supposed to keep her from all harm. She should be the one who grows up healthy to bury her parents.

When one "fails" at this, when the child dies, the parents may feel that they have failed at their most basic function.

The death of any child is a monumental assault on the parents' sense of identity. Because they cannot carry out their role of preserving their own child, they may experience an oppressive sense of failure, a loss of power and ability, and a deep sense of being violated. Disillusionment, emptiness, and insecurity may follow, all of which stem from a diminished sense of self. And this can lead to the guilt which is such a common feature in parental grief.[4]

Parental guilt can take many forms. Some parents experience survival guilt, the feeling that it's not right that they're still alive and their child isn't. There also can be illness-related guilt, where the parent thinks some personal deficiency caused the child's sickness and death. Some parents experience guilt over the belief that in some unknown way they either contributed to their child's death or failed to protect the child. And some experience moral guilt over the belief that the child's death was punishment for one or both parents' violation of some moral or religious code.[5]

Because of all these losses, grief over the death of a child will be more intense and last longer than grief over the loss of anyone else. The death of a child has been called the ultimate bereavement.

A parent who has lost a child will struggle continually with anger at what happened, anger at anyone they feel could have prevented it, anger at the unfairness of what transpired, anger at the disruption of their lives and anger at God. The anger will come and go for years.

Bereaved parents will have to "grow up with the loss." Parents tend to mark their lives by the accomplishments and events involving their children. The dates when those events would have occurred will still come around, even though their child won't be there to experience them. The sixth birthday; the first teen birthday; the times when the child would have received a driver's license, graduated, married and had children—all these things will bring a resurgence of grief when the parents least expect it.

Following the death of a child, a marriage tends to flounder. It's as though the very structure of family life is under attack. Parents may have to intervene with their other children as they react to the loss of their brother or sister. The parents may struggle with vocational pressures because of being distracted and absent from their job for an extended period. Because of their grief, daily routines seem overwhelming, and they may pick at each other when one sees things left undone. There could be a new financial burden because of the child's illness or the unbelievably high expense of a funeral. All these elements add to marital tension.

It's estimated that 90 percent of all couples who lose a child face some kind of marital struggles within the first year after the death. The divorce rate is very high among couples who have lost an only child.[6] Statistics also show that in approximately 70 percent of the families where a child was killed violently, parents either separated or divorced.[7] Many marriages that dissolve after such an experience were held together by a slim thread to begin with, and this event seemed to shred the remaining strands. It also could be that the parenting roles were more intense than the marital relationship itself. But the death of a child does not have to lead to divorce. With the right approach, this tragic experience can become a time of mutual comfort, support and growth.

No parent is ever prepared to lose a child, regardless of the cause of death or the child's age. Ronald Knapp gives us an insightful description of shadow grief, which is often experienced by parents who have lost a child:

Shadow grief reveals itself more in the form of an emotional "dullness," where the person is unable to respond fully and completely to outer stimulation and where

normal activity is moderately inhibited. It is characterized as a dull ache in the background of one's feelings
that remains fairly constant and that, under certain circumstances and on certain occasions, comes bubbling
to the surface, sometimes in the form of tears, sometimes not, but always accompanied by a feeling of sadness and a mild sense of anxiety. Shadow grief will vary
in intensity depending on the person and the unique
factors involved. It is more emotional for some than for
others.

Where shadow grief exists, the individual can never
remember the events surrounding the loss without feeling some kind of emotional reaction, regardless of how
mild.[8]

The Effects on Surviving Siblings

When a child dies, parents are thrust into a multiple-crisis
dilemma—not only are they dealing with the loss of their child,
they are struggling with responding to and dealing with the
remaining children. In some cases, they also have to deal with
the grief of their own parents who have lost a precious grandchild. It is therefore not unusual that the siblings often have to
cope on their own, since the parents do not have the emotional
strength to help them.

When a child dies, who should tell the siblings? Should they
be told together or separately? If there is to be an open casket at
the service, should the children view the body? Should they even
attend the funeral, or be left at home? Should they attend the
graveside service or the get-together that follows? How do you
explain death to a three-year-old or a five-year-old? What if you
are unable to answer their questions? I don't know of any parent

who has really thought through these questions ahead of time. But when they are least capable of doing so is when they're called upon to respond.

In the weeks and months following a child's death, what the parents do and don't do, and what they say and don't say will determine how the other children remember their sibling. In the meantime, the parents will continue to struggle. What do they do with the deceased child's pictures? Room? Clothes? Toys? What if they keep the toys for the other children, but the children refuse to play with them? What if the parents want to discard them, but the children want to keep them?

Who helps the children with their grief feelings? Since most parents don't understand how to handle loss or grief, there's very little help available there. It may be others, such as relatives or church workers or a counselor, who will provide the greatest help.

When a sibling dies, children often wonder, *Why did my brother die?* or *What does it mean to be dead?* Too many surviving children have their own grief complicated because of inadequate or overly simplistic explanations from their parents: "Your brother is living up above the clouds" or "God took him." The child then begins to wonder, *If God took him, will He take me?* Or the parents may give an overly complicated explanation, such as, "Your brother succumbed because of an inflammatory distress response." Since few adults outside the medical profession fully comprehend such a statement, it's easy to see why children would become more confused than ever upon hearing such an explanation.

There is, of course, the old standby parental response, which basically is nothing more than a cop-out: "We'll talk about it another time." Overly simplistic, overly complicated or cop-out responses like these cause more damage, rather than bring healing.[9]

When a sibling dies, what do the other children remember?

Do they think of the good times they shared together? Not often. Instead, the clearest memories seem to be the times they argued, shouted, hit, slapped or got each other into trouble. As a result, they create excessive burdens of guilt for themselves. They forget the naturalness of these interactions and wish there had been better times.[10]

Birth order once again seems to have some significance in how children handle these situations. Older children feel more guilt over having wished their younger sibling would disappear, while younger children feel more of a burden to replace the deceased child.[11]

Many siblings end up competing with the child who died, especially if their parents glorify the deceased child's abilities, intelligence or goodness. When the surviving children hear about their wonderful dead sibling, they may feel unloved or even jealous. They may feel it's an impossible task to compete with the memory of a dead sibling; this in turn leads to resentment, which leads to guilt.[12]

Unhealthy Parental Responses

There are three very common but also unhealthy responses that grow out of the parents' unresolved grief. The first is a response of silence and secrecy regarding the child's death. This response leaves the remaining children feeling haunted by their deceased sibling. They are made to feel that they have to seal their feelings, positive or negative, toward their lost sibling. If they had an enjoyable close relationship, that bond must stay buried. If they had ongoing, unresolved conflicts, those too must stay buried. The children end up grieving alone and silently.

SILENCE

Why the silence? What is it parents are afraid to talk about? Usually it's blame, the shared feeling that they could have done something to prevent the death from happening. And so children, with their limited understanding and resources wonder why they can't talk about it. They may then conclude that their parents are angry at them and that the sibling's death is their fault. This is especially true if the siblings didn't get along prior to the child's death. And so we end up with a situation where the children won't talk because it would upset the parents, and the parents don't talk because it would upset the children. Everyone is busy protecting themselves, as well as one another.

If the child who died was the favorite, in an effort to prevent damaging comparisons with the other children, the parents may not allow the deceased child's name to be mentioned. I saw a perfect example of this in a movie called *Ordinary People*. Buck was the firstborn who could do no wrong. He died while sailing with his younger brother, Conrad. After Buck died, the mother became very cold and unloving toward Conrad, while the father maintained only a very superficial relationship with him. Conrad soon discovered he could never be what his brother was, and he struggled with his mother's comparisons of the two boys. He lived in a home where his brother's memory was dominant, and his own hurts and sadness were denied expression. His guilt intensified; he failed in school and eventually attempted to take his own life. He finally found the help he needed, not from his family, but from a therapist who helped him unlock his feelings, face them and grieve in a healthy way. Conrad was much like many children who live in a home where there is no communication between the family members, nor is there a healthy support system for grieving.

Years ago I saw a 25-year-old man in counseling. As we met together, I discovered that his brother, a Marine, had been killed seven years earlier. I asked him if he and his brother had been close. His reply was, "Yes, we were very close." I also learned that his mother had turned his brother's room into a shrine by keeping it exactly as it was when he was alive. Nothing had been discarded or changed. I asked this man if he had cried over his brother's death. He responded, "Oh, yes, at his funeral." Had he visited the gravesite? Again, he replied, "Yes, at his funeral." But he had neither cried nor been back to the grave for seven years, blocking all emotional expression and grief during that time.

I suggested he take the family picture album, which was filled with pictures of himself and his brother, and visit his brother's grave. He could sit there for a while, reflect on their lives together, pray and see what might happen. He did so, and when I saw him two weeks later he said,

> I went to my brother's grave and did what you suggested. I looked at our pictures and had a lot of memories come back. I prayed and even talked out loud to my brother. It was kind of strange. But after three hours, I cried. Oh, how I cried for him!

I asked him how this felt, and he said, "It felt good. It was a long time coming." I wonder how many there are today who need to cry for a brother or sister.

OVERPROTECTION

A second common but unhealthy response to the death of a child is a fearful, overprotective reaction on the part of the parents. Because one child has died, the fear of losing another one begins to dominate a parent's thoughts. The manner in which the first child died may reflect the parent's response toward the other children. If the child died of a massive head injury from riding a bicycle, the parents may restrict bike riding to going to and from school or only when accompanied by a parent, and even then the child must wear a double-padded helmet. A parent's fears can be transferred to the other children as they sense the apprehension in the parent's life. Some children make it a point to prove they will not follow in their dead sibling's footsteps. Some even become risk takers to prove their invulnerability.

REPLACEMENT

A third common but unhealthy response is a replacement reaction. Sometimes the surviving child or children end up living two lives—their own and that of the deceased sibling. I actually have seen parents appoint a child to step in and begin responding where the deceased child left off. Even older parents who had long since decided against having more children have been known to have another baby as a replacement for the lost child. The replacement position is not an enviable one since the new child most likely will be compared in many ways to the deceased child. This is a difficult burden for any child to carry, trying to live out his or her own identity as well as that of the deceased sibling. The conflictual feelings arising from this burden only add to the child's pressure. The replacement child may have been very close to the sibling, but now because of the pressure exerted by the parents, he or she may alternate between love and hate toward the deceased sibling.[13]

Some adult siblings take it upon themselves to try to fill the hole in their parents' lives by constantly being available or even trying to emulate their dead sibling.

Other Factors Affecting Survivors

Several other factors impact the lives of the surviving children: What was the intensity of death? If a child actually sees a brother or sister die, it may bring on a lasting trauma. The event may always be remembered but not talked about. Whether it be witnessing an accident or observing the last moments of a sibling's life on a deathbed, the event is damaging. Consider the impact of a child discovering a sibling floating facedown in a swimming pool or seeing a sibling struck by a car.

But even if the death occurred elsewhere and the children learned of it secondhand, there still are problems. What actually happened to their sibling is left to their imagination, particularly if there is no opportunity to view the body. This could lead to denial of the loss, especially with very young children who struggle with understanding death and its finality.

Another factor that impacts siblings is the length of time it took for their brother or sister to die. When a child takes years to die because of some insidious disease, the other children feel helpless, abandoned and perhaps overburdened. Because the parents are giving their time, energy, love and attention to the dying child, there is little left for the others. The other children are put on hold for the time being, and may have to assume some parental chores around the house.

An ever common factor is the feeling among remaining children that they could have done something to prevent the loss. They also may feel that they somehow caused their sibling's death. Since many of the childhood and adolescent deaths outside of illness are considered accidental, there is plenty of room for these questions. In *Ordinary People,* Conrad could never be sure that he had done all he could to save his brother from drowning. Many children struggle with the thought that the sibling's death might have been prevented. These children live with guilt, self-blame and even the haunting question, "Do I deserve to be here?"

The age of children at the death of a sibling is critical. Younger children are more likely to misunderstand or to distort a death. Perhaps a young child was so angry at his brother that he secretly wished he would disappear. And then the brother dies. The child believes it happened because he wished for it to happen, so the sibling's death becomes the child's personal responsibility. It's common for a child to believe that what he or she did, said or thought caused the death. Some children live with this distortion for years.[14]

Losing a Sibling as an Adult

What happens when you lose a sibling as an adult? It's been said there is no other loss in our adult life that is so neglected, even though most of us will experience this at some time. In fact, sibling losses may outnumber any other losses. My mother experienced the loss of her six siblings before she died. There's an assumption that the loss of a parent or spouse is the most distressing, but for some adults sibling loss is the hardest.

If you are close in age to your sibling when he or she dies as an adult, you will experience many of the same losses as if this event had occurred in childhood. One of the features of sibling death, and one you need to expect, is that there will be less social recognition of the significance of this loss. The loss may not have the same impact on other members of your immediate family as it does on you. If you have other siblings, they may respond quite differently to the loss than you do.

Why is this loss so significant? Consider John. He had two brothers, one who was two years older and one who was two years younger. Their parents died when the brothers were in their mid to late twenties, which is also the time when they all married. So by the time John was in his fifties, he'd had his parents for half of his life and his wife for about half of his life. But when his older brother died, he lost someone who had been a part of his life from the very beginning. John's future with this brother was gone. No longer would they share the memories, family traditions or birthdays. A constant was gone from John's life. His brother's death made him feel older and much more mortal. His family of origin had shrunk by a third. He found himself wondering if he too would die when he reached the age his brother was when he died. The bell that tolls for a sibling may keep on tolling with the message, "You're next."

> *One of the features of sibling death, and one you need to expect, is that there will be less social recognition of the significance of this loss.*

Just as guilt can come to a child who loses a sibling, it can come to adults, perhaps for different reasons. It may begin with remembering how close you were when you were younger. Then you find yourself wishing you had done more to perpetuate that closeness, but you didn't, and now it's too late. Or maybe there were unresolved issues that you now wish you had settled. Perhaps you wonder why your sibling died first, which activates survival guilt. All of this may be compounded with the additional loss of not being included in decisions about the funeral and other arrangements, because all of that was left to the surviving spouse and children.

If your sibling had a terminal illness, you may experience old rivalries as time, attention or financial resources of parents and others are directed toward that sibling. This and other issues can generate resentment, which later may come back to haunt you after your sibling dies. The obvious door to guilt opens wide.

With a sibling gone, the roles and relationships with other family members may need to undergo a change. This too may entail more loss and stress, as it did in Ted's case. Ted was the second of two sons, and he lived in the shadow of his older brother. After his brother died, he received more attention and recognition for his achievements, but he also had to assume his deceased brother's role of being responsible for his elderly parents.[15]

Perhaps the various aspects of losing a sibling as an adult can best be described by a woman who lost her younger brother, Bob:

> I grieved now for Bob, my brother, who was not only a member of my family but someone who knew me, who understood me, who felt with me, in a way no one else on this planet ever did or would. Someone who, more than I had ever dared know, was me. My brother-double.
>
> And I grieved, too, still more deeply, for all that now would never be. For except in brief, nervous flashes, my brother and I had never been able to truly convey to each other the emotional kinship between us. We had never really been able to express it, enjoy it, sustain each other through it, make anything of it in our lives. We may have wanted to—and I think, as we grew older, that both of us truly did—but we just couldn't manage it. There had

been too much history between us, too many cruel gibes and long silences, too much fear. And that was why, whenever we said hello, we were already edging away, already saying good-bye.

And when I finally understood all of this, fully and deeply, I was able to forgive both of us the chance we had missed with each other and would never have again. Given who we were, and given the world in which we found ourselves, Bob and I had done the absolute best we could. And as that recognition deepened within me over the next weeks and months, I felt my grief lifting. A measure of peace and energy returned to me. And unexpectedly, as the pain receded, I began to feel Bob's presence more vividly. While before I had been able to think of my brother only with sadness and longing, I was now beginning to remember him also with amused affection, to be able to enjoy memories of his con-man charm, his absurdist humor, his breathtaking, unstoppable energy.

I did not stop missing my brother then. I still miss him greatly, and I expect that I always will. But sensing Bob's spirit nearby—chortling, manic, ready for the next high-stakes game—helps me fill the space where he once was.[16]

You Can Prepare

You may already have lost a sibling. If not, you probably will in the future. If you begin to prepare for this now, learning as much as you can about loss and grieving, and then work toward building a better relationship with your siblings, you will deal more effectively with the situation when it comes, be able to remember with a feeling of satisfaction the relationship you shared and then move on with your life in a healthy manner.

Notes

1. Marion Sandmaier, *Original Kin* (New York: E.P. Dutton, 1994), pp. 207, 214, adapted.
2. Al Martinez, "A Shadow on the Moon," *Los Angeles Times,* November 11, 1998, Section C, p. 1, adapted.
3. Carol Staudacher, *Beyond Grief* (Oakland, Calif.: New Harbinger, 1987), pp. 100, 101, adapted.
4. Therese A. Rando, Ph.D., *Grieving: How to Go On Living When Someone You Love Dies* (Lexington, Mass.: Lexington Books, 1988), pp. 164, 165.
5. Ibid., p. 105, adapted.
6. Staudacher, *Beyond,* p. 109, adapted.
7. Ronald J. Knapp, *Beyond Endurance: When a Child Dies* (New York: Schocken, 1986), p. 184, adapted.
8. Ibid., p. 41.
9. Therese A. Rando, ed., *Parental Loss of a Child* (Champaign, Ill.: Research Press, 1986), p. 328, adapted.
10. Katherine Fair Daniel, *Recovering from the Loss of a Sibling* (New York: Dodd, Mead and Co., 1988), p. 2, adapted.
11. Rando, *Parental,* p. 323, adapted.
12. Daniel, *Recovering,* p. 4, adapted.
13. Stephen Bank and Michael Kahn, *The Sibling Bond* (New York: Basic Books, 1982), pp. 270-77.
14. Ibid., pp. 270-82, adapted.
15. Therese A. Rando, *Grieving,* pp. 154-58, adapted.
16. Sandmaier, *Original,* p. 224.

Chapter Eleven

A Change in Your Future

Sibling relationships change. Believe it or not, they really do, although the change may be slow and subtle. In fact, changes occur throughout our life span—whether for better or worse. And like most changes we make in life, changes in sibling relationships often are precipitated by crises. Some of the changes that may take place within a sibling relationship include the amount of time spent together and feelings of acceptance, closeness or even resentment. Surprisingly, it seems that those sibling relationships that are least likely to change are those with either a very close or very troubled relationship.

Let's think about all the various changes or transitions we experience in adulthood. Some are predictable; some are unexpected and sometimes devastating. Perhaps you've experienced one of these transitions already. Consider how the following situations could affect sibling relationships.

Siblings leave home to work or go to school. They marry and move thousands of miles away. Children are born; parents retire and eventually may move in with a sibling or into a nursing home. But what does it do to sibling relationships when a parent dies prematurely or has a lingering terminal illness, or they divorce? If the divorce occurs when the siblings are still at home, there is the possibility of remarriage and the inclusion of stepsiblings, which can be a major adjustment. A sibling may become incapacitated, contract a serious illness or die. What happens when one of them announces he or she is gay? A sibling may divorce, have an affair, be discovered as a child abuser or become a substance abuser. Even a job promotion or job loss can impact everyone.

A transition, just like a crisis, carries with it two possibilities. It can become a time of growth and opportunity, or it can become a time of disruption. Some transitions provide siblings with the opportunity to repair, revitalize or enhance the relationship. But other transitions reinforce existing rifts and conflicts. Sometimes close relationships have been severed by a transition. Whatever happens as a result of transitions or crises depends upon the amount of investment the siblings have in the relationship.[1]

The Marriage Effect

Perhaps the event that produces the greatest change in sibling relationships is marriage. An intimate new relationship such as marriage requires reshuffling of family connections. In the classic book *Little Women* by Louisa May Alcott, one of the characters, 16-year-old Jo, is upset when she learns that her sister Meg, a year older than she, is considering marriage. Quite unhappily she states, "I just wish I could marry Meg myself and keep her safe in the family." When it seems certain that Meg is going to marry, Jo tells a friend, "You can't know how hard it is for me to give up Meg." Later she says, "It can never be the same again. I've lost my dearest friend."[2]

Marriage is not a step closer to your family of origin; it's a step away. Loyalties are being transferred. Each person who marries brings baggage in the form of family members. Take, for example, Frank and June. Frank, the oldest of five siblings, brought his brothers and sisters, as well as his parents, into a marriage with June, who brought two siblings, two stepsiblings, a mother and stepfather and a father and stepmother. Some of the first major issues facing a newly married couple is where to spend Thanksgiving and Christmas and whether or not they all should get together for each sibling's and each parent's birthday. These issues can become quite complicated.

A JUGGLING ACT

Many try to maintain their sibling bonds while adding the new ones. For most, the juggling act becomes a struggle, to say the least. It is inevitable that you will lose some companionship and availability when your sibling marries. You lose some of the interaction you had, as well as the intensity of the relationship. Your sibling's first priority has become his or her spouse. Your spontaneity changes. You can't just drop in unexpectedly like you used to. Some siblings feel replaced. Someone else has come in and taken your sibling away, and there's an empty space. Often what develops is a postmarital intimacy gap with siblings. You may make or hear statements like the following:

- We never get together anymore.
- I don't know her that well anymore.
- We don't even talk on the phone like we used to.
- What I miss are the outings where the three of us would take off for the weekend.

The more time siblings spent together, and the closer they were while growing up, the more likely they will feel abandoned when one of them marries. Sisters seem to experience this more than brothers, or at least they more readily voice their loss.[3]

We all would like to think we're in charge of the selection process of whom we marry. But are we? There are many influences that enter into such a decision, including those of siblings. As one author said, "What makes siblings' influences on marital choice so significant is that they are more common and powerful than we imagine, and we generally are unaware of their consequences."[4]

SPOUSE/SIBLING STRIFE

What happens if your siblings don't approve of your selection? How much voice do they have? What if parents also disapprove?

Siblings are more likely to object to a sibling's choice when the potential partner is different in terms of social, ethnic or religious background. Conflict occurs when the two people who marry have a different perspective of the value of adult sibling relationships. Different sibling styles create tension for the newly married couple. If the close sibling starts to drift away, who will be blamed, the sibling or the new spouse?[5]

Numerous problems can occur with siblings and in-laws. I've seen cases where people feel their spouse is more married to siblings than to them. More time, attention and even money is invested in the sibling relationships than in the marriage. You can imagine the feelings of resentment and jealousy this provokes. This leads to accusations, demands, quarreling and comparisons.

Is there any one in-law who is more likely than anyone else to become a problem? Dr. Evelyn Duvall's study on in-law relationships was presented in her book *In-Laws: Pro and Con*. She states that mothers-in-law are considered the number one object of complaints. There are usually more conflicts between the man's mother and his wife than anyone else. But coming in second place are sisters-in-law. And generally speaking, it appears that the most troublesome sister-in-law is the sister of the husband.

In this study some of the sisters-in-law showed "tendencies to meddle, criticize, to be dependent, to be possessive, to pamper and intrude." These sisters-in-law seem to have the same difficulty in letting go of their brothers as some mothers do in letting go of their sons. The difficulty they struggled with was very basic: They had a hard time sharing their brother with any other woman—even when that woman was his wife. The sisters assumed the role of being an objectionable type of mother figure.

Sister-in-law difficulties include negative behavior such as competitiveness, rivalry, tattling, boasting, unfriendliness, coldness and being critical—all of which seem to have their roots in childhood sibling rivalry. If the patterns of bickering, comparing and belittling continue into adulthood, newcomers (spouses) become fair game for these responses as well. And sometimes disagreements are battled out through the in-laws rather than between the main combatants.[6] This adds fresh fuel to the fire of changing sibling relationships.

Sibling rivalry, which we discussed in earlier chapters, emerges at the time of a wedding. A marriage can feed any existing competition between siblings. Statements like the following actually have been made by competitive siblings:

- Well, I married first, so you'll just have to sit and wait.
- Guess who gave our parents the first grandchild!
- I hate to say it, but my wedding was the classiest and the largest!
- So, how many wedding gifts do you think we received?

- I think I ended up with the pick of the litter. You can only hope you do as well someday.

Frozen Relationships/Frozen Memories

As you can see, sibling relationships have various reasons to change. One or more members of a family might change their lifestyles and patterns of behavior in adolescence or in adulthood. But there are some sibling relationships, whether positive or negative, that remain stuck no matter how much one person tries to change. It's as though they are frozen in time.

One sibling's identity can become stuck or frozen because of another sibling's death. If the sibling who died had been idolized, his or her image usually remains untarnished and may be passed on to the next sibling. A classic example of this is found in our own history. Joseph Kennedy, Jr. was the oldest son of former ambassador Joseph P. Kennedy, Sr. After Joe Jr. died in World War II, the next son in line, John, took up his brother's hero position. John then went on to fulfill the dream his father had for Joseph by becoming president of the United States of America. During his first term of office, however, he was assassinated. Then the next son, Robert, also was assassinated as he sought to climb the political ladder.

Not only can relationships and identities become frozen, but so can perceptions and misunderstandings. You can have two siblings remember the same childhood event, but their stories are so different you wonder about their sense of perception. One sibling may have a frozen image of what another sibling was like as a child, and no matter what anyone says to the contrary, that sibling's mind is made up. A sister remembers herself as being kind to her brother, but the brother remembers her as being cruel. If the atmosphere in the home was chaotic and dysfunctional, it's more likely that family members will have frozen mis-understandings and images of one another. In a dysfunctional home, there is very little certainty about anything, which contributes to feelings of insecurity. But if there is at least one certainty about something or someone within the family—even if it is a negative certainty—it helps to relieve tension and anxiety and makes it easier to accept a negative image of a sibling than that of a parent. So these images become frozen. If something or someone comes along and attempts to defrost those images, any sense of certainty and security is threatened.[7]

Do you want changes in your sibling relationships? If so, what are those changes? Is this a mutual desire between you and your siblings, or is it just yours? How will you go about instituting these changes?

The Effects of Childhood Roles

The United Nations is known for its peacekeeping or peacemaking ventures. They try to heal rifts between nations, so warfare won't erupt. Often in families the pattern of warfare has been ongoing for decades, so what's needed is more of a mission to stop the existing war and establish peace, rather than simply trying to prevent future wars.

Perhaps you come from a family in which very little needs to be improved. If so, be thankful. If not, remember that resolving problems with your siblings is almost as important as resolving problems with your parents. I've seen fathers look at their children and see what they disliked about one of their siblings. I've seen wives relate to their husbands in the same way they related to their siblings, and on and on.

Current unresolved issues often can be traced back to the roles siblings played as children. Dr. Patricia Love suggests some interesting and insightful questions to help gain greater insight into sibling relationships. Let's imagine that all of your family of origin members are alive and you're all together at a family reunion. You're all interacting, and someone takes a photo of you. What would each person be doing? Who is sitting or standing next to whom? How much space is there between the various individuals? Who is touching one another? Would anyone be left out of the photo? What emotions would you see? Do any roles come to mind as you describe this picture?

Now let's assume you and your siblings are living on an island. Place your house where you would be most comfortable. Now, place a house for each sibling. Who lives the closest and who lives the farthest from you? Are there windows in your house, and which houses do your windows face? Where are the paths leading from your home, and to which homes do they connect? If a brother or sister had to move in while their home was being repaired, which one would you choose? If your parents came to visit, which child would they stay with first? How long would they stay with each one? Would you or anyone else be jealous? If you had a bicycle on the island, to whom would you feel comfortable lending it?

What do your answers tell you about your sibling relationships? Are you satisfied with them, or do you want to make some changes?[8]

I've had men as well as women tell me, "It's too late. I'll just have to accept the fact that my brother is who he is. Our relationship is cast in cement. It will never change." But it's never too late to improve a relationship with a brother or a sister. Even a good relationship can be improved. I've talked to numerous individuals who felt their relationships were so distant they were beyond repair. But these people were mistaken. They discovered in some cases that the relationships improved because both they and their siblings had changed. Others discovered that their relationships improved even if they were the only ones who changed. Sometimes it was as simple as refusing to participate in the old games anymore.

Some Desired Relationship Changes

I've asked some adult siblings how they wanted their sibling relationships to be different. Here are some of the responses:

- I'd like my sister and me to be equals. I don't want to live in her shadow anymore.
- Friends. That's all. Shouldn't a brother and sister be able to be friends?
- I'd like our family get-togethers to be pleasant. No more bickering. No more trying to outdo the others.
- I want our childhood to be over. We're adults. And we're all Christians. Let's start responding as adult Christians.
- No more jealousies.
- Let's just be cordial. We won't be friends, but we could be civil.

That's the first step—figuring out what you want to be different. How is that done?

Change starts by determining what you can and will do differently. Don't concentrate on fixing your sibling. It's easy to identify what the other person is doing to thwart progress. He or she may or may not change. But you can change your way of responding. After all, we are people who are called to be in the process of changing constantly. God wants every believer to "become conformed to the image of His Son" (Rom. 8:29, *NASB*).

He wants to help us "grow up in all aspects into Him, who is the head, even Christ" (Eph. 4:15, *NASB*).

Changing a relationship involves trying to understand how another person feels about you and, if possible, the reasons for those feelings. You and your siblings are a result of your parents' influence and experiences. You are products of history.

IMPROVEMENT, NOT PERFECTION

Be realistic in working toward a different sibling relationship. Don't look for perfection, work for improvement. The first is unrealistic and unattainable and sets you up for failure. The second is realistic and attainable, even if it involves only minor changes in your own attitude and responses. Of course, it's important to remember that any changes you make could cause the relationship to worsen. It's a chance you take when you choose to change.

A DIFFERENT PARADIGM

Another thing you can do to change relationships is to develop a new way of viewing progress. If you note a 5 percent change in the relationship, but 95 percent stays the same, which percentage will be your focus? Again, you have to make a choice. Think of it like this: Have you noticed the difference between the eating habits of buzzards and bees? Buzzards search for food by flying overhead and looking for dead animals. When they find a decaying animal, they move in to gorge. Honeybees, however, have quite different habits. They look for nectar, which is sweet. They're very discriminating as they fly through the varieties of flowers in a garden. The buzzards and bees each find what they're looking for, but which would you rather have?

What do you look for in your sibling relationships? Even if there's only a 5 percent improvement and 95 percent stays the same, what will you focus on and reinforce? If you focus on the 95 percent, it will cripple any future progress. It's better to focus on even the slightest improvement, to be thankful for it and to reinforce it.

> *What would happen if you identified and wrote down the typical ways you respond to your siblings and then wrote a description of how you might respond differently in the future?*

Changes won't happen unless you invest time, energy and patience. And change probably will happen slowly. I remember what Chuck Swindoll said about this dynamic:

> Change—real change—takes place slowly. In first gear, not overdrive. Like ice skating or mastering a musical instrument or learning to water ski, certain techniques have to be discovered and developed in the daily discipline of living. Breaking habit patterns you established during the passing of years cannot occur in a few brief days. Remember that. Instant change is as rare as it is phony.[9]

It will help everyone if you can learn not to refer to or view your siblings in their old roles. Seeing them as the fixer, the chosen one, the clown, the prodigal, just perpetuates your way of reacting and doesn't allow them the opportunity to change.

Can you shed the role you've been accustomed to playing all

these years? What would happen if you identified and wrote down the typical ways you respond to your siblings and then wrote a description of how you might respond differently in the future? It's possible to do this; others have. It's a way of unhooking from your old roles.

LOSE THE UNIFORM

It's interesting to see how quickly siblings revert back to their old roles when they get together. It's as though each one brings a family uniform with them to wear. The next time you're headed to a family event, leave your uniform in the closet. Better yet, discard it entirely.[10]

I've seen family conflicts that range from constant bickering to not talking to a sibling for years. As varied as these conflicts are, most of them carry the potential for painful wounds.

Many of the hurts we experience are undeserved. During conflict, words are exchanged that can penetrate to the heart. Some words are like arrows in the way they pierce: when the shaft of the arrow is pulled free, the jagged point remains and festers, keeping the hurt alive. If you've been hurt by your sibling for one reason or another, I'm sure you have wished you could reach back to that painful encounter and cut it out of your life.

If you want to move toward reconciliation, there is a three-step process that has worked for many. But before you proceed to that process, there are some important points to keep in mind.

You may think there's been a problem—and there actually may have been a major issue—but your sibling may deny its existence, or claim that he or she had no responsibility for it. In your heart and mind, before you ever begin, give your sibling permission to believe this. How your sibling responds does not determine the validity of your perception, nor the healthiness of your reaching out and attempting to improve a relationship.

Remember that each person probably will have a different memory and slant on past events. That's why some see no value in rehashing what happened in the past. But one or more of your siblings may be responsive to working on a better relationship for the future.

Once you've done all you can to reconcile differences with your siblings, accept the results. They may or may not be what you wanted, but concentrate on the fact that you have reached out to resolve, and that you will no longer participate in the conflict.

Steps to Resolution

What are the steps involved in resolving a relationship with a sibling?

Before you start, sit down with your sibling and clearly state your purpose. Let the sibling know what you want to accomplish. You could make statements like these:

- I'm interested in making our relationship better. I'd like to work toward that, and I hope you will as well.
- I want to talk about our relationship. I've been concerned about how I've been feeling, and I'd like to work on improving things between us.
- I've spent some time thinking about things that happened between us in the past, things that affect the way we respond to each other now. I've been hoping we could work on this together.

SPEAK THE SAME LANGUAGE

The first step to resolution, once you've established your purpose, is to focus on this important principle: *You will have a greater opportunity to be heard if you speak your sibling's language.*

Those who relate best to others and are more influential in being heard are those who have the flexibility to adapt their own communication style to match others. Why? Because people like to talk with others who talk like they do—those who speak their language. Numerous books are devoted to this concept for married couples, as well as for those in business relationships. Why should it be any different for siblings? Some of the most basic relational conflicts are tied into communication.

For example, if your sibling is a detail person, be specific and give details when you talk. But if the sibling prefers bottom-line summaries, give your information in a condensed version rather than providing every detail. If you tend to start sentences and not finish them or jump from subject to subject while your sibling thinks and communicates in a one-two-three linear fashion, give your message in that linear style.

If you are a visual learner, you probably use phrases like the following:

- Do you see what I mean?
- Here's the picture.
- Here's my viewpoint.
- Let's take a look at this project.

If you talk with another person who is visual (most men are), you'll connect in that manner. But if your sibling is an auditory person, you need to rephrase your statements accordingly:

- Do you hear what I'm saying?
- How's this sound to you?
- Let's talk about this together.
- I'd like to hear your thoughts.

If your sibling is a kinesthetic (feeling) learner, be sure to use feeling words:

- I feel about it this way.
- I sense you feel differently.
- Can we discuss our feelings about this?

And speaking of feelings, if you're a woman talking to your brother, instead of asking him how he feels about something, you may get a better response if you ask, "What's your inner reaction or response to this?" (For detailed information on this subject, see *How to Speak Your Spouse's Language* by H. Norman Wright.)

Keep in mind that your personality differences affect the way you communicate. If you or your sibling happen to be an extrovert, bear in mind that extroverts tend to brainstorm out loud. It doesn't mean that what they say is necessarily what they're going to do. They just talk out their thoughts. Extroverts have to work at listening, as it doesn't come naturally for them. Extroverts believe that if they can say just one more thing, it will clear up a conflict. And remember, extroverts need more affirmations and compliments than others.

If your sibling is an introvert, too much talking can wear him or her out. The most important thing to remember about introverts is that they need to think about an answer or response within the privacy of their mind for a while before giving an answer. If your sibling is quiet, it doesn't mean that you weren't heard or that you're being ignored. Encourage your introverted sibling to think about what you said or about your question for a while, and then answer when ready. And don't interrupt if he or she pauses for a few seconds in the middle of the response; it doesn't mean he or she is finished. Last of all, always have your discussion with your introverted sibling in private, since privacy is important to introverts.

Following a few simple guidelines like these can make a difference in how your sibling responds to you.

ACCEPT RESPONSIBILITY

The second step in reaching resolution with your sibling is to accept responsibility for your role in the relationship problems by making statements such as these:

- I know that when we were kids, I got more attention than you did. That must have hurt.
- When you got into trouble, I'd take advantage of it to get what I wanted.
- Did you ever wish we could have our childhood all over again? I do. I was mean and selfish to you. I could have been nicer. You weren't a hard person to get along with.
- When we were teens, I know I got a lot more attention from Dad then you did. I talked more and I was a show-off. I must have been a pain in the neck to you.
- Even now I don't contact you enough. If I were you, I'd feel left out of the loop a lot.
- Sometimes I treat you as I did when we were kids. I don't want to do that anymore. You're not a kid; you've changed.

INDICATE THE DESIRED CHANGES

The third step is to indicate how you would like the relationship to be different, now and in the future. Here are some examples:

- Here is how I'd like to respond to you in the future.
- I'd like us to talk more and feel good about our conversations.

- I'd like us to talk more and not focus on having the last word.
- I want to be closer to you. I intend to call you twice a month. Is that comfortable for you?
- I'd like to build a close, trusting relationship with you. I need someone else in my life to share with, and I'd like it to be you.
- I'd like us to find a way to respond differently at the family gatherings, so we don't let Mom and Dad put us back into our childhood responses.
- I'd like to ask your forgiveness for the way I treated you. I want you to know you can count on me to respond to you in a better way.[11]

Once you've done this, you've taken all the direct steps you can take on your own. There may be a positive, satisfying response from your sibling, or there may not be. The important thing is that you've tried.

FORGIVE

The fourth step in resolving sibling relationships is called *forgiveness*. You've probably been angry or resentful toward a sibling for what he or she said or did. The only way for a new relationship to have a chance is through forgiveness. And that means giving up your hurt.

Forgiveness can be costly. Why? Because you may be dealing with some broken promises. Are you willing to trust again? Remember, forgiveness means that once it is given, a gag order has been slapped on whatever it was that was done. It can't be brought up again in a blaming, accusatory way, to be thrown back in your sibling's face. You need to be sure you understand and accept this before extending forgiveness.

We are all different in the way we handle our hurts. One sibling holds the hurt for months and years, while the other seems to relinquish it in hours. Dr. Lewis Smedes, author of *Forgive and Forget*, put it well when he said:

> Some people are lucky; they seem to have gracious glands that secrete the juices of forgetfulness. They never hold a grudge; they do not remember old hurts. Their painful yesterdays die with the coming of tomorrow. But most of us find that the pains of our past keep rolling through our memories, and there's nothing we can do to stop the flow.[12]

When someone has been offended, there is a lingering hurt. I counsel with a number of people who are consumed with bitterness and resentment. Ephesians 4:31 tells us to put away all bitterness. Do you know what bitterness is like? It's the disposition of a person with a tongue as sharp as an arrow. A bitter person "needles" others and is ready with a sharp and painful reply to siblings. Resentment is a feeling of ill will toward a person. It wants others to make an ongoing series of payments for what they have done.

The problem with being bitter and resentful is that we have allowed what our sibling has said or done to control our emotions and our lives. If we don't release that sibling from whatever he or she has done, we simply enslave ourselves to that hurt. Being chained to hurt and hate from the past means anger and resentment in our future. When we hold onto our hurts, we are misusing the gift of memory.

You have lots of memories with your siblings, and you have a choice about which ones you dwell on. You can choose to use your memory to think about the warm and happy times, or you can choose to use your memory to hurt as you've been hurt. How? By nursing the hurt, keeping it alive and, in some way, perhaps plotting to hurt in return. Memory can be used as a blessing or as a weapon.

Years ago I saw a Western movie in which two antagonists, each clutching his gun, eyed each other from 30 feet away. Their weapons had the power to kill. But instead of using them on each other, each abandoned his weapon, saying, "I will fight no more. There never is a real winner. We've tried fighting. Let's try living." With that, they moved toward each other in peace.

"But," you say, "if I forgive her for what she said, she could do it again." True. Even when we forgive, there are no guarantees the offense won't be repeated.

"If I forgive him, I make myself vulnerable and open to being hurt again." Also true. But forgiveness still is the best alternative to being frozen in hurt because of disagreement. If you want a sibling to pay for an offense and so you withhold contact, use silence, or are blunt, cold or caustic, when is the payment sufficient? And how do you feel about yourself as you respond in this manner? I am not trying to be judgmental or harsh; I simply am concerned over the pain that people have inflicted upon themselves by holding onto hurts from their interaction with others. As Lewis Smedes puts it,

> For two people who are coming together after a falling out, truthfulness requires a promise made and a promise meant to be kept. Those who hurt you must return to you with a promise that they will not hurt you again; and you need to believe that they intend to keep the promise they make. They cannot offer you a guarantee; they cannot be depended on the way you might rely on a computer or a well-trained dog. They are ordinary, fallible

human beings; they are not God. You lay a bet on them; you need to take a risk.[13]

What do you want? Do you want to hang on to that hurt festering inside and slowly build a pool of bitterness? Will you hang on to the pain that will consume your joy and belief in Christ's power and presence? Can you accept your siblings for who they are and what they may have done or said to you? This means forgiving to the point where you no longer allow what has occurred in the past to influence you. Only by doing this can you be free to develop yourself, to experience life, to communicate in a new way, to love yourself and others.

Perhaps Webster's definition of forgetting can give you some insight into the attitude and response you can choose. To forget means "to lose the remembrance of; to treat with inattention or disregard; to disregard intentionally; overlook; cease remembering or noticing; to fail to become mindful at the proper time." Is there a sibling in your life who is suffering from emotional malnutrition because of resentment and unforgiveness?

By not forgiving, we inflict inner torment upon ourselves, making ourselves miserable and ineffective. Forgiveness says, "It's all right; it's over. I no longer resent you nor see you as an enemy. I love you, even if you can't love me back." When you forgive someone for hurting you, you perform spiritual surgery inside your soul; you cut away the wrong that was done to you so that you can see your former "enemy" through new eyes that can heal your soul. Detach that sibling from the hurt and let the hurt go, the way children open their hands and let a trapped butterfly go free. Then invite that person back into your mind, fresh, as if a piece of history between you had been erased, its grip on your memory broken at last.[14]

We are able to forgive because God has forgiven us. He has

given us a beautiful model of forgiveness. Allowing God's forgiveness to permeate our lives and renew us is our first step toward wholeness. If you want to come to the place that you can wish your siblings well in all areas of their lives, you have to take the step of forgiveness.

At the same time, we must remember that forgiveness is a process, not an event. Restoring a relationship is also a process, just like healing. And no matter who takes the first step to rebuild the relationship, you and your sibling may have mixed feelings. It's not uncommon to want to draw closer to your sibling, while at the same time feeling threatened by that closeness. The timing for how fast the rebuilding occurs will vary with each individual involved.

If you have genuine regrets about something that occurred in the past, the words "I'm sorry" are an important and necessary ingredient for resolving those regrets. Saying these words doesn't constitute an admission to being a bad, evil person. In effect, you are actually saying, "I wish I could rewrite that part of the past, but I can't. I am responsible for this, and you can count on that not happening again."

RECONCILE

Another important step in resolving unhealthy relationships with your siblings is reconciliation. Unfortunately, some people lump forgiveness and reconciliation together. But they are separate issues. Forgiveness is unilateral, something you do whether or not the other person participates or responds. Forgiveness is your choice. It's under your control.

Reconciliation is different. It requires mutual participation. One person can't do it alone. It takes two who are in sync with one another, at least to some degree. Both sides have to want reconciliation to happen. Both individuals need to accept responsibility for having contributed to the problem, and then they need to work through the process of repentance and forgiveness together.

> *Forgiveness is unilateral—something you do whether or not the other person participates or responds. Reconciliation requires mutual participation—two who are in sync with each other, at least to some degree.*

In the story of the prodigal in Luke 15, there was reconciliation between the father and the youngest son, but not between the two brothers. The older brother held on to his resentment toward his brother. Not only that, but he also resented his father for accepting his brother back. The father tried to reconcile with his older son, but it appears the older brother resisted reconciliation on all counts.[15]

Is it possible for reconciliation to take place between you and your sibling? Reconciliation is always possible, but let's look at what is required for that to take place.

First, the individuals involved must understand that forgiveness is nothing that can be earned, it must be given. You can't buy back a relationship. Author Dave Stoop said, "The beauty of both forgiveness and reconciliation is that they are free actions that come from the heart."[16]

Reconciliation also is connected to something besides forgiveness—acceptance. For reconciliation to happen, acceptance must be mutual. But acceptance costs, and it involves several features:

- Both parties have to be able to accept each other, including strengths and weaknesses.
- Both need to be willing to admit their own failures.
- Both must desire healing for the broken relationship.
- Both have to be willing to give up the "right" to be right.
- Both have to be willing to give up any desire for revenge or retribution.[17]

RESPOND

There is one final step to consider when attempting to change a sibling relationship for the better. How will you respond to your sibling if he or she accepts your overtures? Perhaps you hadn't considered that. It could be you'd be so surprised at the response—particularly if it's a positive one—that you wouldn't know exactly what to say or do.

I have seen some who were like the prophet Jonah. Remember his response when the people of Nineveh repented? Jonah was upset because the people responded to God's message. He actually wanted them to reject the message so God would judge them! I've seen family members react like this when a sibling becomes a different person and responds in a new way. Why? Because the old ways of interacting with this changed sibling no longer work. The family members are now forced into some sort of change themselves, and that makes them uncomfortable. In addition, if the sibling has changed for the better, the rest of the family no longer can complain about the sibling's former behavior patterns. They have lost their basis for a poor relationship!

The Word of God gives a practical example of the way God wants us to respond when people change. In the early chapters of this book, we discussed the story of a favorite son, Joseph. Do you remember that after Joseph was sold into Egypt, he eventually attained a position of power? In time, he and his brothers reconciled and the brothers, their families and their father came to live with Joseph. (See Genesis 37–50 for the entire story.) Their father requested that upon his death he be taken back to the land of Canaan to be buried. After his death and burial, Joseph's brothers became concerned that Joseph might exact retribution from them for what they had done to him years earlier:

> When Joseph's brothers saw that their father was dead, they said, "What if Joseph holds a grudge against us and pays us back for all the wrongs we did to him?" So they sent word to Joseph, saying, "Your father left these instructions before he died: 'This is what you are to say to Joseph: I ask you to forgive your brothers the sins and the wrongs they committed in treating you so badly.' Now please forgive the sins of the servants of the God of your father." When their message came to him, Joseph wept (Gen. 50:15-17).

Chuck Swindoll describes the brothers' reaction:

> They still couldn't appropriate grace. It was still "too good to be true." Everything they had said and done so many years ago came rushing back into their minds. Fear also returned as their imagination took charge. Had Joseph been kind to them only for their father's sake? Was that the reason he had not yet taken his revenge upon them?

There was no doubt in their minds that the death of their father could mean the sudden removal of a restraining influence on their brother. As long as Jacob was there, they felt safe, or at least safer. With him gone, who knew what might happen?[18]

But note Joseph's response, which is a good pattern for each of us:

> But Joseph said to them, "Don't be afraid. Am I in the place of God? You intended to harm me, but God intended it for good to accomplish what is now being done, the saving of many lives. So then, don't be afraid. I will provide for you and your children." And he reassured them and spoke kindly to them (vv. 19-21).

Joseph wasn't punitive toward them. He didn't gloat over them. He didn't make them squirm. He didn't activate their guilt. He simply reassured them.

Can you reassure your siblings? Joseph spoke kindly to his brothers. Will you choose to do the same? What was the key ingredient in Joseph's response? It was grace. A simple word and a loving response—*grace*.

Joseph was led by grace. He spoke by grace. He forgave by grace. He forgot by grace. He loved by grace. He remembered by grace. Because of grace, when his brothers bowed before him in fear, he could say, "Get on your feet! God meant it all for good."[19]

And when we walk in grace, we can say the same about our own sibling relationships: God meant it all for good.

Notes
1. Marion Sandmaier, *Original Kin* (New York: E. P. Dutton, 1994), pp. 184-87, adapted.
2. Louisa M. Alcott, *Little Women* (Boston: Little, Brown and Co., 1915 [1880]), pp. 253, 292.
3. Sandmaier, *Original,* pp. 188-92, adapted.
4. Dr. Jane Greer with Edward Myers, *Adult Sibling Rivalry* (New York: Crown Publishing, 1992), p. 151.
5. Sandmaier, *Original,* pp. 190-92, adapted.
6. Evelyn Millis Duvall, *In-Laws: Pro and Con* (New York: Association Press, 1964), pp. 221, 241, 256ff, adapted.
7. Stephen Bank and Michael Kahn, *The Sibling Bond* (New York: Basic Books, 1982), pp. 80-90, adapted.
8. Dr. Patricia Love, *The Emotional Incest Syndrome* (New York: Bantam Books, 1990), pp. 185-87, adapted.
9. Charles Swindoll, *Come Before Winter . . . and Share My Hope* (Portland, Ore.: Multnomah Press, 1985), pp. 131, 132.
10. Sandmaier, *Original,* pp. 240-44, adapted.
11. Love, *Emotional,* pp. 190-93, adapted.
12. Lewis B. Smedes, *Forgive and Forget* (San Francisco: Harper & Row, 1984), p. XI.
13. Ibid., p. 34.
14. Ibid., p. 37.
15. David Stoop and James Masteller, *Forgiving Our Parents, Forgiving Ourselves* (Ann Arbor, Mich.: Vine Books, 1991), pp. 264-67, adapted.
16. Ibid., p. 268.
17. Ibid., p. 269, adapted.
18. Charles R. Swindoll, *Joseph* (Nashville: Word Publishing, 1998), p. 202.
19. Ibid., p. 204.